HIGHLIGHT'S CULINARY SERIES

CHINESE DIMSUM RECIPES

HILIT PUBLISHING CO., LTD.

AUTHOR: MADAME TUAN-HSI SHOU

Madame Shou, a culinary artist, is also the author of "Chinese Homemade Dishes of Four Seasons," "Chinese Seafood," "Easy-made Chinese Dishes," and "Chinese Healthy Recipes." Her ability is such that she now teaches in several cooking schools. The wife of Mr. Kang Feng, the captain of the Desserts Dept. of the Hoover Restaurant, Madame Shou is also an accomplished painter and calligrapher having studied under the late Mr. Lung-an Chun, an outstanding artist. Madame Shou's mother, Madame Chu Shan, is also a famous painter and it is this literary and artistic environment that has led to Madame Shou's dishes being not only delicious, but also elegant and delicate.

Copyright 1983
by Hilit Publishing Co., Ltd.
Taipei, Taiwan, Republic of China

All rights reserved. No part of this publication may be reproduced in any form by any means without the prior permission of the publisher.

National Central Library Catalog Card Number: 427.16/8347
Hilit's General Item Number: HILIT 00048
Hilit's Classified Item Number: C006-E

Sixth Edition June 1994

Publisher: Dixson D.S. Sung.
Author: Tuan-hsi Shou
Photographer: Kun-hon Lin and Jenn-yu Chen
Translator: Chun-chi Chen and Li-min Yang
Lithographed in Taiwan, Republic of China

PREFACE

Owing to the change of social structure, people have learned to pay attention to culinary art. Besides regular meals, snacks and desserts also play important roles in our daily life.

A lot of people can not resist the temptation of those delicious and lovely desserts arrayed in the bakery and supermarket. Many of them like very much to know how to make those desserts at home. But they could not find a good recipe. In this cookbook, we collect more than 100 recipes of the most popular Chinese snacks and desserts. We are confident that by following the simple steps with pictures illustration, you'll be able to make various kinds of snacks and desserts for your family. We also believe that these desserts and snacks can bring you an even better life.

It's our wish to help every woman to be a successful wife. Your success at home is our greatest satisfaction.

Dixson D.S. Sung
President of
Hilit Publishing Co., Ltd.

FOREWORD

Most Western desserts and snacks are very fattening. For people who are overweight and people who have heart disease, those desserts and snacks are taboos.

The utensils used to make Western desserts and snacks are complicated. The Chinese way of making desserts and snacks is different. Though we do not have various kinds of utensils, we can still make various kinds of delicious desserts and snacks with simple ingredients.

Many housewives are troubled by the method of preparing dough for different kinds of pastries. They do not know how much flour to use for the number of servings.

This book offers simple methods to solve these problems. We introduce 109 recipes for Chinese snacks and desserts. You will find them easy to make, money-saving, and tasty.

CHINESE DIMSUM RECIPES

CONTENTS:

1. Flour and Noodles

A. How to make dough.................6-7

Chicken E-Mein Soup........................8-9
Bean Noodles Broth.........................8-9
Homemade Bean Threads.................8-9
Tao-Hsiao-Mein in Beef Brisket Soup...............10-11
Pork Sauce Macaroni......................10-11
Wu-Lung Noodles in Seafood Soup.........12-13
Mein-Hsien (Thin Noodles) in
Sesame Oil Chicken Soup...................12-13
Chow-Yiu-Mein, Taiwanese Style............14-15
Yang-Chun-Mein...........................14-15
La-Mein in Special Sauce..................16-17
Ta-Lu-Mein................................16-17
Chow-Mein, Cantonese Style................18-19
Curry Beef Chow-Mein.....................18-19
Wonton, Wenchou Style....................20-21
Peanut-Flavored Stone Biscuits............20-21
Cat's Ears................................22-23
Flour-Fish Soup...........................22-23
Cake of Turnip Shreds.....................24-25
Milk Pancakes.............................24-25
Salted Vegetable Patties..................26-27
Red Bean Pancakes........................26-27
Steamed Shao-Mai.........................26-27
Kuo-Tieh (Fried Dumplings)................28-29
Shuei-Chiao (Boiled Pork Dumplings).......28-29

B. How to make scalded dough.........30-31

Leek Ho-Tzu (Leek Boxes)..................32-33
Scallion Pancakes.........................32-33
Homemade Vegetable Pancakes.............34-35
Grilled Ground Meat Pancakes..............34-35
Steamed Dumplings........................36-37
Doubled Pancakes.........................36-37

C. How to make leavened dough........38-39

Steamed Small Pork Buns..................40-41
Steamed Juicy Pork Buns..................40-41
Steamed Pork and Vegetable Buns.........40-41
Hua-Chuan (Steamed Bread Twists).........42-43
Man-Tou (Steamed Bread)..................42-43
Ying-Su-Chuan (Steamed Shredded Rolls)...44-45
Layered Cake.............................44-45
Po-Su Buns...............................46-47
Easy-to-Make Rolls.......................46-47
Steamed Cake.............................48-49
Sponge Cake, Cantonese Style.............48-49
Smiling Muffins..........................50-51
Chiao-Kuo (Crunchy Fritters).............50-51
Huo-Shao................................52-53
Grilled Pork and Vegetable Buns..........52-53

D. How to make oiled dough...........54-57

Curry Dumplings..........................58-59
Red Bean Mash Pastry.....................60-61
E-Kuo Pastry.............................60-61
Chrysanthemum Pastry.....................62-63

Wheel Pastry.................................62-63
Shao-Ping Sandwiches........................64-65
Shao-ping (Baked Cakes).....................64-65

2. Rice...................................66-67

How to prepare bamboo leaves................66-67
Tsung-Tsu (Glutinous Rice Dumplings),
Hu-Chow Style...............................68-69
Red Bean Mash Tsung-Tzu, Hu-Chow Style......68-69
Chien Tsung.................................70-71
Spiral Tsung-Tzu............................70-71
Kuo Tsung...................................72-73
Ho-Fen Rolls (Rice Rolls)...................72-73
Ho-Fen Soup.................................74-75
Sushi, Two Different Styles.................74-75
Black Mushroom and Pork Tsung-Tzu,
Taiwanese Style.............................76-77
Mi-Kao (Rice Cake)..........................76-77
Yiu-Fan (Oiled Rice)........................76-77
Congee, Cantonese Style.....................78-79
Taro Congee.................................78-79
La-Ba Congee................................80-81
Salted Ba-Jen Congee (Salted Congee with
Eight Ingredients)..........................80-81
Ba-Bao Rice.................................82-83
Sweet Mi-Kao (Sweet Rice Cake)..............82-83
Rice Pudding in Bowl........................84-85
Leavened Rice Cake..........................84-85
Hot Rice Noodles, Chiang-Hsi Style..........86-87
Stir-Fried Rice Noodles, Taiwanese Style....86-87
Salted Mi-Tai-Mu............................88-89
Mi-Tai-Mu and Assorted Ingredients with Chopped Ice..88-89
Sweet Nien-Kao (Year Cake)..................90-91
Turnip Cake, Cantonese Style................90-91
Grilled Nien-Kao............................92-93
Stir-Fried Nien-Kao with Vegetable..........92-93
Tang-Yuan (Balls of Glutinous Rice) in Osmanthus and
Fermented Rice Soup.........................94-95
Fried Glutinous Rice Balls..................94-95
Pork Tang-Yuan..............................96-97
Yuan-Tzu Soup...............................96-97

3. Assorted Dishes

Squid Broth.................................98-99
Fried Oyster Patty..........................98-99
Sweet Potato in Sugar Syrup.................100-101
Seafood Rolls...............................100-101
Yiu-Tou-Fu (Fried Bean Curd) and
Bean Threads Soup...........................102-103
Fried Lung-Fang-Tuei........................102-103
Hot and Spicy Fen-Pi Soup...................104-105
Cold-Blended Liang-Fen......................104-105
Peanut Soup.................................106-107
Fried Sesame Balls..........................106-107
Chun-Bing (Spring Rolls), Two Different Styles......108-109
Tempura.....................................108-109
Jou-Yuan (Pork-Stuffed Balls) Taiwanese Style.......110-111
Grilled Oyster Paste........................110-111
Fried Yu-Kuo (Taro Cake)....................112-113
Fried Taro Sticks...........................112-113

4. Cold Desserts..........................114-115

How to make gelatin and pudding.............114-115
Banana Gelatin..............................116-117
Pineapple Gelatin...........................116-117
Egg Pudding.................................118-119
Creamy Egg Pudding..........................118-119

Notes:
1. Unless otherwise specified, each recipe serves 4 to 6.
2. The English title of this book is "Chinese Dimsum Recipes" because the Chinese call snacks and desserts dimsum or dien-hsin.
3. There are three kinds of flour mentioned in this book: all-purpose flour, plain wheat flour, and cake flour. The main difference among them is that all-purpose flour is the richest in protein and cake flour has the least amount of protein. This is why pastries made with all-purpose flour are more elastic than those made with plain wheat flour; and pastries made with plain are more elastic than those made with cake flour. To get the best results, we suggest you use the type of flour specified in each recipe. You can use all-purpose flour if other kinds of flour are not available.

麵食類

Noodles and Watered Dough

How to make dough

1. (A) Whether the dough should be wet or dry, the average amount of flour to use is about ½ cup per person—for example, use 2 cups of flour for 4 people. Of course, this is subject to change according to the appetites of the people who are going to be served.
   (B) After measuring, sift the flour carefully into a large container. If it is for leavened dough, sift three times to make sure that the flour mixes well with the other ingredients.
2. Make a well in the middle. Add water to it slowly, stirring with a fork or chopsticks. You can add 1 tablespoon of lard to make the dough smooth and shiny.
3. Keep adding water till the flour turns into small lumps.
4. Flour your hands lightly. What follows is hand work.
5. Hand work is the literal meaning of kneading and rubbing the lumps into a dough.
6. Soak a piece of clean gauze or cheesecloth in water, then wring it dry.
7. Cover the dough with the wet gauze. Let it stand for 20-25 minutes. This step is called Hsing-Mein, or "to let the dough wake up." The purpose is to let the flour become completely moistened by the water.
8. If you want the pastries to be very elastic, remember to apply the hand work of kneading, pulling, and pushing, whether it is a leavened or scalded dough.
9. If you don't want your pastries to be very elastic, apply the method of pressing and cutting as frequently as possible.
10. The longer you knead, pull, and press, the smoother and tenderer the pastry dough will be. Otherwise, it will feel grainy and rough.
11. If you are not experienced at making dough, adding the correct amount of water might be a problem. If the dough is too wet to knead, just put some flour to one side and add little by little while kneading till the dough is moderately soft.
12. If the dough is too dry and is hard to knead, just cut it open or make some cuts on it, sprinkle on some water, and knead. Repeat till the dough is firm enough.
13. Keep kneading the dough till it is very smooth; then you can start making pastries. If you are not in a hurry to do so, just cover it with a piece of wet cloth.

Notes:
1. Generally speaking, the ideal proportion of water to flour is 1 to 3.
2. Beaten egg can replace some of the water to make the pastry more nutritious.

燉雞湯伊麵
CHICKEN E-MEIN SOUP

Ingredients:
2 chicken legs, 4½ cups cold water, 1 tablespoon ginger wine, 10 ounces E-Mein.
(I) 1½ teaspoons salt.

Method:
1. Wash the chicken legs and cut into 1-inch pieces. Cook in boiling water for 1 minute and remove to a casserole bowl before adding cold water and ginger wine. Put in a steamer to steam for 40 minutes, remove and add ingredients (I).
2. Cook E-Mein in boiling water for ½ minute and drain before adding to the chicken soup. Serve.

肉糖豆簽
BEAN NOODLES BROTH

Ingredients:
1½ ounces dried lily flowers, 4 tablespoons sliced fish stock, 4 coils Chinese bean noodles.
(I) 8 cups cold soup stock, 2 tablespoons cornstarch.
(II) ⅓ cup shredded black mushrooms, ¼ cup shredded lean pork, ¼ cup shredded bamboo shoot.
(III) 1 tablespoon soy sauce, 2 teaspoons salt, ½ tablespoon sugar.
(IV) 2 tablespoons chopped parsley and scallion, some sesame oil.

Method:
1. Remove footstalks from the dried lily flowers and soak in water for about 10 minutes. Drain.
2. Blend ingredients (I) well. Bring to the boil over medium heat, add the lily flowers, sliced fish stock, and ingredients (II) and return to the boil.
3. Put in Chinese bean noodles and ingredients (III). Use chopsticks to loosen the noodles. Sprinkle ingredients (IV) on the soup, take off the heat and serve.

Notes:
1. Chinese bean noodles are made from bean starch, you can buy them in Oriental markets.
2. You can use instead E-Fu-Mein, which is first steamed, then fried.

家常豆絲
HOMEMADE BEAN THREADS

Ingredients:
5 ounces green bean starch, 16 ounces rice flour, 4 tablespoons oil, 3 tablespoons sliced scallions, 8 cups soup stock.
(I) ⅓ cup shredded pork, ¼ cup shredded squid (soaked), ¼ cup shredded fungus, ¼ cup shredded green vegetable, ¼ cup shredded bamboo shoot.
(II) 1½ teaspoons salt, 1 tablespoon soy sauce, 1 teaspoon sherry.

Method:
1. Mix the green bean starch thoroughly with rice flour adding enough water to make a thick paste.
2. Grease a skillet thoroughly. Pour in the paste and shake the skillet to spread the mixture in a thin layer. Cook over a low to medium heat, turning it over to cook on both sides but do not let it get scorched. Remove and let it cool before cutting into long threads.
3. Pour oil into a frying pan. Stir-fry the sliced scallion briefly, add ingredients (I) and (II) and continue to stir-fry. Add the stock and bring to the boil before putting in the green bean threads to cook for another 3 minutes. Remove and serve.

Notes:
1. Pepper, parsley and red chili pepper can be added according to your wish.
2. Another way to cook green bean threads is boiling. Or you can stuff green bean wrappers with a filling and deep-fry them.

牛肉湯刀削麵
TAO-HSIAO-MEIN IN BEEF BRISKET SOUP

Ingredients:
1¼ pounds beef brisket, 3 cups plain wheat flour.
(I) 1 slice ginger, 1 scallion (sliced), ½ tablespoon aniseed, ½ tablespoon cumin, 1 mangosteen, 3 tablespoons sherry, 1 teaspoon salt.
(II) 2 tablespoons chopped scallion, 1 tablespoon parsley, ½ teaspoon pepper.

Method:
1. Wash the beef and cut into 1-inch cubes. Cover with boiling water and cook for 1 minute. Remove and rinse.
2. Wrap the spices in ingredients (I) in a piece of cheesecloth. Bring 15 cups of water, the brisket, salt, sherry, and the spice bag to the boil. Then turn the heat down to low and simmer till the beef is well cooked. Discard the spice bag but preserve the rest.
3. Knead flour with enough water to make a stiff dough then cover with a piece of wet cloth and let it rest for 20 minutes before you knead again till it is very smooth. Shape it into a long, rounded pillow.
4. Bring a pot of water to the boil. Add 1½ teaspoons salt. Holding the dough in one hand, slice it with a knife into ribbon-like noodles about ⅓" wide. Cook the noodles in boiling water for 1 minute, ladle out and put them in the beef soup. Bring it to the boil and cook for another 2-3 minutes. Remove and serve, sprinkled with ingredients (II).

Note:
Be sure to make your dough a little stiff and dry so it will be easy to cut and more elastic to eat.

辣肉醬炒通心粉
PORK SAUCE MACARONI

Ingredients:
1 pound macaroni, 4 tablespoons oil, sliced cucumber, onion rings.
(I) 8 ounces lean ground pork, 1 tablespoon hot bean paste, 2 teaspoons chopped chili pepper, 1 cup soup stock.
(II) 1 teaspoon salt, 1 teaspoon sugar, ½ tablespoon ginger wine, 1 tablespoon chopped scallion.

Method:
1. Bring a pot of water to the boil and add 1 teaspoon salt. Put in the macaroni and cook for 7-8 minutes before draining and then rinsing under cold running water.
2. Put oil in a frying pan. Stir-fry ingredients (I) and (II) till it all smells good then add the macaroni and stir-fry till evenly mixed. Remove.
3. Garnish with cucumber slices and onion rings.

Notes:
1. You can choose any type of macaroni you like, since various kinds are suitable.
2. Another way of cooking macaroni is to bake boiled macaroni with grated cheese and sauce on top.

海鮮烏龍麵

WU-LUNG NOODLES IN SEAFOOD SOUP

Ingredients:
5 ounces shrimps (shelled), 1 sea crab, 1 squid head (soaked), some dried black mushrooms, 1 sea cucumber, 8 clams, 4 ounces lean pork, 6 cups soup stock, 3 tablespoons sliced stock fish, 4 quail eggs, 4 packs Wu-Lung noodles.
(I) 1 teaspoon salt, 1 tablespoon ginger wine, ½ teaspoon pepper.

Method:
1. Wash the shrimps, remove the intestines, and rinse. Rinse the crab and cut into pieces, rinse the squid and cut into 1″ pieces, trim footstalks from the dried black mushrooms and soak the caps in water, rinse the sea cucumber and slice it, open the clams with a knife and rinse, and slice the pork.
2. Put the soup stock in a saucepan. Add the fish, pork, black mushrooms, quail eggs, and sea cucumber and bring to the boil. Add the noodles, crab, and ingredients (I) and boil for 2 minutes before adding the shrimps, squid, and clams. Boil briefly and serve.

Note:
Remove any scum from the surface during cooking.

麻油雞麵線

MEIN-HSIEN (THIN NOODLES) IN SESAME OIL CHICKEN SOUP

Ingredients:
4 chicken legs, 4 ginger slices, 1 bundle mein-hsien, 6 tablespoons black sesame oil, 2 tablespoons rice wine, 6 cups water.

Method:
1. Rinse the chicken legs and cut each into 4 pieces.
2. Cut the mein-hsien with scissors into long sections and put them on a piece of cloth on a plate. Bring a cup of water in a steamer to the boil and steam the mein-hsien for 2 minutes.
3. Put the sesame oil in a frying pan. Fry the ginger for a while, add the chicken pieces, and stir-fry till the color changes. Add the wine and water and bring to the boil and before adding the mein-hsien. When soup returns to the boil, serve.

Note:
Leave the mein-hsien in the steamer until you want to stir-fry it. Rinse it gently before cooking.

台式炒油麵
CHOW-YIU-MEIN, TAIWANESE STYLE

Ingredients:
2 cups plain wheat flour, ¼ cup all-purpose flour, 1 teaspoon baking soda, 1½ cups water, 5 ounces bean sprouts, 10 ounces fresh oysters (without shells), 4 tablespoons cornstarch, 3 tablespoons sliced scallion, 4 tablespoons oil, ½ cup shredded pork, ½ cup shredded Chinese Cabbage.

Seasoning:
1 tablespoon ginger juice, ⅓ teaspoon five-spice powder, 1½ teaspoons salt, 1 tablespoon soy sauce, ½ teaspoon pepper, ½ teaspoon sherry, ½ cup soup stock.

Method:
1. Sift the flours together. Dissolve the baking soda in the water and knead into the flour to make a yellowish dough. Let it stand for 20-25 minutes, and then use a noodle maker to make the dough into yiu-mein (oiled noodles).
2. Cook the noodles in boiling water for 1-2 minutes, drain and mix in a tablespoon of oil.
3. Trim root parts from the bean sprouts, rinse, and drain. Wash the oysters with water mixed with a little salt, picking out any impurities. Rinse off the salted water under running water. Drain. Add cornstarch to the oysters and mix well.
4. Bring a pot of water to the boil. Add the oysters and cook for ½ minute before removing and rinse with cold water.
5. Pour oil into a frying pan. Stir-fry the sliced scallion till it smells good, and then add the pork and stir-fry till the color changes. Add the shredded Chinese cabbage and stir-fry till softened before putting in the bean sprouts, yiu-mein, and seasoning. Stir-fry briefly, then simmer, covered for 1 minute. Remove the cover, stir-fry briefly, and serve.

Note:
This dish can be made with leftover yiu-mein.

陽春麵
YANG-CHUN-MEIN

Ingredients:
1 teaspoon salt, 16 ounces green vegetable.
(I) 2 cups plain wheat flour (or 16 ounces machine-made noodles).
(II) 10 ounces pig's bones, 1½ ounces small scallops, 10 ounces chicken feet, 1 slice of ginger, 1 scallion (sliced), 1 tablespoon sherry, ½ teaspoon salt, 12 cups water.

Method:
1. Wash the pig's bones. Soak the scallops in water for a while, and then brush off any sand before soaking in water again for 4 hours. Remove and crush. Wash the chicken feet and cut each into 2 pieces.
2. Put ingredients (II) in a pot. Boil till liquid is reduced by a third then turn off the heat. Strain the liquid into a clean bowl.
3. Mix the flour with some water and knead into a dough. Press it flat with a noodle machine or roll into a large flat piece, and then cut the piece into noodles.
4. Bring a large pot of water to the boil, add the salt, then the noodles, and then boil for 1 minute. Remove to a serving bowl and pour on the broth.
5. Rinse the green vegetable, trim off old and withered parts, and cut into pieces. Boil in water and put on top of the noodles.

Notes:
1. When making this dish, remember to make more soup than noodles.
2. Machine-made noodles are very soft and easily cooked. They are suitable for children and people with digestive ailments.

雜醬拌麵
LA-MEIN IN SPECIAL SAUCE

Ingredients:
Cold boiled water, 5 tablespoons oil.
(I) 2½ cups all-purpose flour, ¼ cup cake flour, Water (about 104°F) (or 1⅓ pounds ready-made la-mein).
(II) 2 tablespoons broad bean paste, 2 tablespoons sweet bean sauce, ½ tablespoon soy sauce, 1½ tablespoons chopped scallion, ½ tablespoon soy sauce,1½ tablespoons chopped scallion, ½ tablespoon sugar, 5 ounces water.
(III) 8 ounces diced pork, 3 tablespoons diced cucumber, 3 tablespoons diced carrot, 4 tablespoons diced salted vegetable root, 4 tablespoons diced bamboo shoot.
(IV) 2 tablespoons peanut oil or sesame oil.

Method:
1. Mix the two kinds of flour together, kneading with enough warm water to make a soft dough. Cover with a piece of wet cloth and let it stand for 20 minutes before kneading again thoroughly to make the dough elastic.
2. Lightly flour the dough. Shape it into a long roll and then wind the roll around two rolling pins. Pull apart slowly in opposite directions the distance depending on your strength. Let it go slack, and wind around and pull again. Keep winding and pulling till the roll becomes threads. Remember to flour the roll every time before you wind and pull. (There is a labor-saving way to make la-mein: Fix one rolling pin so it doesn't move, and pull out the dough with the other rolling pin.).

3. Bring a pot of water to the boil and cook the la-mein for 1-2 minutes. Add a little cold water and bring to the boil again before ladling out and soaking in cold boiled water till cool. (In winter, this step can be omitted.) Drain. Blend well with ingredient (IV).
4. Pour oil into a frying pan. Stir-fry the mixed ingredients (II) first till it all smells good, and then add ingredients (III) and cook for 3 minutes. Remove and blend with la-mein. Serve.

Notes:
1. Other kinds of noodles can be used to replace la-mein.
2. In summer, after blending the la-mein with oil, you can refrigerate it. Blend with some sauce before serving.
3. If you want to make sure that the noodles are cooked, pick up one thread, break it, and examine the cross section. If it is white in the center and transparent around, the noodle is done.
4. If you like a strong taste, increase the amount of seasoning or add ½ teaspoon of chopped chilli pepper.

打滷麵
TA-LU MEIN

Ingredients:
8 ounces pork, 3 ounces fungus, 6 tablespoons oil, ½ tablespoon chopped scallion and garlic stem, 10 slices carrot, 10 large cucumber slices, 8 cups clear broth (made from pig's bones), 2 tablespoons cornstarch paste, 2 eggs (well beaten), 16 ounces noodles (la-mein, chieh-mein, or tao-hsiao-mein).

Seasoning:
(I) 1½ tablespoons soy sauce, 1 teaspoon salt.
(II) 3 tablespoons sesame oil, 1½ teaspoons pepper.

Method:
1. Cut the pork into big, thin slices. Rinse the fungus and cut into 1″ squares.
2. Put oil in a large frying pan. Stir-fry the chopped scallion and garlic stem till they smell good and then add the sliced ingredients. Add seasoning (I) while stir-frying; 1½ minutes later, pour in the clear broth. Bring to the boil, add the cornstarch paste slowly to make the soup creamy. Turn off the heat. When the soup cools down a little bit, pour in the egg batter and stir-slightly.

3. Bring a pot of water to the boil and add the noodles. When cooked, ladle out the noodles and place in a soup bowl, and then pour in the creamy soup. Sprinkle with seasoning (II). Serve.

Note:
La-mein are the noodles pulled into strips from dough. Chien-mein are like vermicelli, freshly made and cut with a knife. Tao-hsiao-mein are ribbon-like noodles cut with knife.

廣式炒麵

CHOW-MEIN, CANTONESE STYLE

Ingredients:
5 eggs, 2½ cups plain wheat flour, ⅔ cup oil, 10 ounces green-stemmed flat cabbage, several dark mushrooms, 8 ounces cha-shao-jou (barbecued pork), 1 ounce shelled shrimps, 5 ounces oiled chicken, 5 ounces roasted duck, 10 slices of cucumber, several slices of bamboo shoot, several quail eggs, 1 tablespoon sherry.

Seasoning:
(I) 1½ teaspoons salt, ½ teaspoon white pepper.
(II) ½ teaspoon salt, ½ teaspoon soy sauce, 2 tablespoons cornstarch paste, ⅓ cup soup stock or water.

Method:
1. Beat the eggs lightly; there shouldn't be too many bubbles. Mix slowly with flour and then knead to form a dough. Cut the dough into noodles with a noodle machine.
2. Bring a pot of water to the boil and cook the noodles till half done. Ladle, cut and soak in cold water till cool, and then drain. Blend evenly with 2 tablespoons of oil.
3. Rinse cabbage, remove old and withered stems and leaves, and cut into 2"x⅓" strips. Rinse the mushrooms and cut into wide shreds.
4. Grease a large frying pan with 6 tablespoons of oil. Put in the noodles and stir to loosen with chopsticks. Put in seasoning (I) and stir-fry thoroughly. Coil the noodles before adding 4 tablespoons of oil slowly along the rim. Cover and fry (not stir-fry) till the noodles become browned, and then shake the pan. When the noodles no longer stick to the bottom, turn the other side up. Add another 4 tablespoons of oil, as before. Fry till a little scorched. Remove to a serving plate keeping the remaining oil in the pan.
5. Put the barbecued pork, cabbage, mushrooms, shrimps oiled chicken, roasted duck, cucumber slices, bamboo shoot slices, shelled quail eggs, and seasoning (II) in the pan and stir-fry for 1 minute before sprinkling with sherry. Turn off the heat.
6. Put the stir-fried mixture on the noodles. Serve.

Notes:
1. In Cantonese style, the noodles have to be fried till both sides are browned.
2. Egg noodles are crispy and delicious, but require more oil.
3. If you choose the ready-made E-Fu noodles, use following cooking method: Put 4 tablespoons of oil in a large frying pan. Stir-fry scallion and garlic stem till they smell good. Add green-stemmed flat cabbage and mushrooms. Stir-fry briefly. Pour in a cup of soup stock, salt, soy sauce, and coiled noodles. Simmer, covered. When the soup is boiling, add the barbecued pork then pour in the cornstarch paste. Bring to the boil again and serve.
4. Cha-shao-jou, oiled chicken and roasted duck are all cooked items which can be bought in Cantonese restaurants.

咖哩牛肉炒麵

CURRY BEEF CHOW-MEIN

Ingredients:
10 ounces spinach, 1½ teaspoons salt, 3 cups plain wheat flour, 10 ounces beef, 6 tablespoons oil, 1 large onion (sliced into 1" pieces), 1½ cups soup stock, 3 ounces snow peas (trimmed).
(I) 1 tablespoon cornstarch, ½ egg white, 1 tablespoon ginger wine.
(II) 4 tablespoons chopped red scallion head, 1 tablespoon chopped ginger and garlic.
(III) 5 tablespoons curry powder, ½ cup milk, ½ teaspoon salt, 1½ tablespoons sugar.

Method:
1. Remove old and withered stems and leaves from the spinach and pick out about 2 ounces of tender leaves to mince. Rub the rest with salt in a basin till the green juice oozes out.
2. Blend the minced spinach with the green juice, and then knead it into the flour to make a green dough, adding water if necessary. Cut the dough into noodles with a noodle machine, or you can roll out the dough to a big, thin piece, flour the surface, fold it into a 5"-wide strip, and then cut into noodles with a knife.
3. Rinse the beef and cut into 1" cubes, and then marinate with ingredients (I) for 20 minutes.
4. Bring water to the boil and boil the noodles for 1½ minutes. Drain.
5. Put oil in a frying pan. Fry ingredients (II) for a while, adding the onion and ingredients (III), then the beef slices. Stir-fry till the color of the beef changes, and then add the noodles and soup stock. Let it boil for 2 minutes before adding the snow peas. Stir-fry for 1 minute and serve.

Note:
Red scallion heads are the root parts of a kind of scallions which are red on the surface.

溫州大餛飩
WONTON, WENCHOU STYLE

Ingredients:
5 ounces shelled shrimps, 5 ounces lean ground pork, 6 tablespoons chopped green-stemmed vegetable, 4 tablespoons diced spiced bean curd, 4 tablespoons diced egg pancake, 10 ounces thick wonton skins (or 8 ounces thin ones), 8½ cups soup stock (mixed with 1 teaspoon salt), 6-8 tung-hao or spinach.
(I) 1 teaspoon salt, ¼ teaspoon white pepper, ½ tablespoon ginger wine.
(II) ⅓ cup shredded salted vegetable root, ⅓ cup shredded laver, ⅓ cup shredded egg pancake, ⅓ cup chopped scallions.

Method:
1. (A) Shrimp and pork filling:
   Rinse the shrimps, drain, mince with the ground pork, and blend well with ingredients (I).
   (B) Pork and vegetable filling:
   Sprinkle salt on the chopped green-stemmed vegetable, squeeze dry, mince with the ground pork, add the diced spiced bean curd and egg pancake, and blend well with all of ingredients (I) except the ginger wine.
   (C) Vegetable filling:
   Use the ingredients in filling (B) except ground pork. Add 2 teaspoons of sesame oil and 1½ teaspoons of sugar.
2. Spread ½ tablespoon of filling on a wonton skin and pinch the four corners together gently; or place the filling on one corner, fold the skin up to make a triangle, and then pinch together the two outer corners; or fold into a square pillow shape (mostly for the one with vegetable filling).
3. Bring the soup stock to the boil. Add the wontons and boil for 1 minute. Put in tung-hao or spinach (which has been washed clean and torn into 1″ pieces). Cook briefly and serve.
4. Add ingredients (II), sesame oil, and pepper to increase the flavor.

Notes:
1. There are big wonton skins and small ones. The former are used in this dish.
2. To make an egg pancake, beat eggs till smooth. Heat oil in a large frying pan (do not let it get too hot). Pour the egg batter in gently so that it forms a thin layer in the pan. It is done when it is no longer runny.

花生石頭餅
PEANUT-FLAVORED STONE BISCUITS

Ingredients:
2 cups plain wheat flour, ¾ cup cake flour, 3 tablespoons sugar, ½ teaspoon salt, ½ cup peanut powder.

Method:
1. Blend the ingredients well. Mix with enough water to make a hard dough.
2. Spread stones in a large frying pan. Heat over a high flame. When the stones are hot enough to immediately vaporize water sprinkled on them, reduce the heat to medium.
3. Divide the dough into several parts and roll out each to a circle. Place one by one on the hot stones and bake till crisp and hard. (Do not turn.) Remove and let cool on a wire rack.

Note:
While making stone biscuits, you can blend stir-fried flour with uncooked flour or use peanut powder or sesame powder instead.

貓耳朵
CAT'S EARS

Ingredients:
1¾ cups plain wheat flour, ½ teaspoon salt, 6 tablespoons shelled shrimps, 2 teaspoons cornstarch, 10 ounces spinach, 4 tablespoons oil, 6 tablespoons sliced lean pork, 8 cups soup stock.
(I) 4 tablespoons sliced fungus, 6 tablespoons sliced fresh squid.
(II) 2 teaspoons salt, 1½ teaspoons ginger wine.

Method:
1. Knead the flour with salt and enough water to make a dough and then let it stand for 20 minutes. Knead again till very smooth and divide into 3 or 4 parts.
2. Roll each part into a long strip, then cut into 1″ squares. Pinch each square into the shape of a cat's ear.
3. Rinse the shrimps and drain before adding cornstarch and blending well. Remove old and withered parts from the spinach, wash, and cut into 1″-wide strips.
4. Pour oil into a frying pan. Put in the sliced pork and stir-fry till it smells good and then add the stock and bring to the boil. Put in the cat's ears and boil for another 2 minutes. Add ingredients (I) and (II) and the shrimps and spinach, bring to the boil and serve.

Note:
You can alter the soup ingredients as you wish.

撥魚
FLOUR-FISH SOUP

Ingredients:
4 tablespoons oil, 9 cups soup stock, ¼ cup shredded carrot, 2 cups shredded green-stemmed flat cabbage.
(I) 2 cups plain wheat flour, ⅓ teaspoon salt.
(II) ¼ cup shredded pork, ¼ cup shredded bamboo shoot, 2 tablespoons shredded scallion.

Seasonings:
(I) 1½ teaspoons salt, 1 tablespoon soy sauce.
(II) ½ teaspoon pepper, 1 tablespoon sesame oil.

Method:
1. Mix ingredients (I) with enough water to make a bowl of paste and let it stand for 15 minutes before blending again thoroughly to make the paste smooth and grainless.
2. Put oil in a large frying pan. Stir-fry ingredients (II) till they smell good; then add the stock and shredded carrot and bring to the boil.
3. Tilt the bowl of paste slightly and use a chopstick to put the paste in the boiling soup, bit by bit. When the slices pile up in the pan, separate them with a spatula. After all the slices are in the pan, add the shredded cabbage and seasoning (I) and boil for another 2 minutes. Remove and serve.
4. Sprinkle seasoning (II) on top.

Note:
You can add eggs into the paste to make it more nutritious, but it will be less elastic in texture.

蘿蔔絲餅
CAKE OF TURNIP SHREDS

Ingredients:
3 cups plain wheat flour, 4 tablespoons dried baby shrimps, 1½ cups shredded turnip, 2 garlic stems, 2 tablespoons oil, 4 tablespoons chopped pork, 1 cup oil, 1 tablespoon cornstarch paste.
(I) 1 teaspoon salt, 1 teaspoon sugar.
(II) 1 teaspoon salt, ½ teaspoon pepper.

Method:
1. Knead enough water into the flour to make a moderately soft dough and divide into 8-10 pieces.
2. Rinse the shrimps and soak in water for 10 minutes, chopping and then blend the shredded turnip with ingredients (I) and let stand for 20 minutes. Squeeze dry. Slice the garlic on a slant.
3. Pour 2 tablespoons oil into a frying pan. Stir-fry the shrimps and chopped pork till they smell good, add the shredded turnip, garlic, and ingredients (II) and stir-fry well. Add cornstarch paste to thicken. (The mixture should be sticky.) Remove and divide into 8-10 parts.
4. Roll each dough piece into a thin pancake. Place the filling in the center of each pancake and wrap up before shaping into patties.
5. Pour 1 cup of oil into frying pan. Heat to over medium-hot, lower the heat, and place the patties in the pan. Cook, turning once, until the crust becomes browned and slightly scorched

Notes:
1. You can skip the step of stir-frying and just blend cornstarch with raw ingredients for filling.
2. You can use Chinese cabbage and bottle gourd to replace the turnip.

鮮奶餅
MILK PANCAKES

Ingredients:
1½ cups milk, ½ cup sugar, 2 cups plain wheat flour, 1 tablespoon butter.

Method:
1. Put the milk and sugar in a small saucepan. Heat, stirring, over a low flame to melt the sugar, and then add the flour and stir to a smooth paste. Let stand for 20 minutes and mix again.
2. Grease a frying pan with butter. Follow, using either of the two methods below.
   (A) Heat the pan. Put in a tablespoon of the batter, shake the pan so the batter swirls into a circle and bake over low heat. When the batter is no longer runny, remove. Serve by itself or with jam.
   (B) Heat the pan, add the batter, shake the pan as above and bake over low heat. When the pancake is still soft but no longer runny, turn and cook on the other side. Remove and roll it up to eat.

Note:
If you do not like sweet food, use water instead of milk and salt instead of sugar. Use to wrap scrambled egg or shredded vegetables.

鹹菜餅 SALTED VEGETABLE PATTIES

Ingredients:
3 cups plain wheat flour, ⅓ cup shredded lean pork, 3 tablespoons oil, ½ cup salted vegetable, ⅔ cup oil.
(I) 1 tablespoon soy sauce, ⅓ teaspoon salt, ⅔ tablespoon sugar, 2 teaspoons ginger wine, 1½ teaspoons cornstarch powder.
(II) ½ teaspoon pepper, 2 tablespoons cornstarch paste.

Method:
1. Blend flour with enough water to make a smooth dough and then divide into pieces of 4-5 ounces each. Shape each into a patty 2″ in diameter and 1″ thick.
2. Marinate the shredded pork with ingredients (I) for 20 minutes. Pour 3 tablespoons of oil into a frying pan and stir-fry the pork till the color changes. Remove, leaving the juice in the pan. Add the salted vegetable, stir-fry till it smells good and then add the shredded pork again and stir-fry for a while. Add ingredients (II) to make the dish creamy. Remove.
3. Place 1½ tablespoons of filling in the center of each round piece. Pinch the edges together carefully, and then flatten each one slightly and gently.
4. Pour ⅔ cup of oil into a frying pan. Fry the patties over low heat, turning to cook on both sides. Fry till the surface is scorched and crisp. Serve.

Note:
All fried food should be drained on absorbent paper or it will taste greasy and unpleasant.

豆沙餅 RED BEAN PANCAKES

Ingredients:
8 ounces red beans, ⅔ cup oil.
(I) ⅓ cup shortening or lard, 10½ ounces brown sugar, 2-3 tablespoons water.
(II) 2¾ cups plain wheat flour, ½ teaspoon salt, 1-2 tablespoons lard.

Method:
1. Check the red beans for any impurities, cover with 2 inches of water and soak for 4-6 hours.
2. Drain the beans, bring a pot of water to the boil and add the beans and cook till they split open. Drain, let cool, and put into a food processor with ½ cup of water. Mash. Pour the mashed beans into a clean cheesecloth bag, tie tightly, and then press out the moisture. The mashed red bean is ready when it is no longer wet.
3. Put ingredients (I) in a frying pan and boil over a low heat. When the sugar melts and the mixture becomes shiny and brown, add the mashed red bean. Over a medium flame, stir till half the water evaporates. (The red bean paste should be dark red and smell good.) Remove and divide into 2½ ounces balls.
4. Blend ingredients (II) with some water and knead to a smooth dough and then cut into 4-ounce pieces. Shape each piece into a ball, flatten, and then roll into 1″-thick wrapping skin before placing a red bean ball in the center and pincking the edges together carefully.
5. Fry as in Salted Vegetable Patties.

Notes:
1. If a food processor is not available, put the cooked red beans in a clean cloth bag. Tie tightly. Soak the bag in water. Rub the bag with your hands in the water till the bean skins are crushed and the beans are mashed. Let the bag stand still for a while. Pour off some water when the mash settles. Pack into another bag, then press out the moisture.
2. With crushed skin, the red bean mash is more nutritious but less smooth.

燒賣 STEAMED SHAO-MAI

Ingredients:
13 ounces very lean ground pork, 24 medium to large shelled shrimps, 24 pieces wonton skin (or dumpling skin).
(I) 1 teaspoon salt, 1 tablespoon ginger wine, ½ teaspoon pepper.
(II) 1½ teaspoons ginger wine, 2 teaspoons cornstarch.

Method:
1. Blend the ground pork well with ingredients (I) and let it stand for 20 minutes. Rinse the shrimps and marinate with ingredients (II) for 20 minutes.
2. Place 1½ tablespoons of filling in the center of each wonton skin. Pinch the edges up to make a flower pattern leaving a hole in the center to let the filling show a little bit. Place a shrimp in the center.
3. Place shao-mai in a steamer and steam for 25 minutes. Serve.

Note:
If you do not like shrimps, you can use quail eggs instead.

鍋貼
KUO-TIEH (FRIED DUMPLINGS)

Ingredients:
3 cups all-purpose flour (or use ready-made dumpling skins), 10 ounces lean ground pork, ⅓ cup chopped chives, ¼ cup oil, ⅓ cup water.
(I) ⅔ teaspoon salt, ⅓ teaspoon pepper, 1½ teaspoons ginger wine, 1½ teaspoons sesame oil.

Method:
1. Mix flour with enough water to knead into a smooth dough and roll into a long roll as wide as your thumb. Cut into 1″ pieces, and then flatten and lightly flour each piece and roll into a round skin that is thick in the center yet thin at the egges.
2. Blend the ground pork and chopped chives with ingredients (I). Put 2 teaspoons of this filling in the center of each wrapper and pinch the edges up making sure that the bottom of each dumpling should be flat.
3. Pour oil into a frying pan. Heat slightly. Arrange dumplings in the pan and fry over medium heat for 1 minute before turning the heat to high and adding the water. Fry over medium heat with the cover on. When the water is absorbed and there's a sizzling sound, remove the lid. Remove the dumplings when the bottom of the dumplings are slightly scorched.

Note:
You can add 110°F water to the flour to make the dumpling skin more elastic and soft.

水餃
SHUEI-CHIAO (BOILED PORK DUMPLINGS)

Ingredients:
10 ounces Chinese cabbage (or leek, chive, turnip, or white Chinese cabbage), 13 ounces lean ground pork, 3 cups all-purpose flour (or 20 ounces ready-made dumpling skins).
(I) 1 teaspoon salt, 1 teaspoon sugar, ½ teaspoon white pepper, 1 tablespoon ginger wine, ½ tablespoon sesame oil, ⅓ cup water or soup stock.

Method:
1. Rinse the Chinese cabbage and blanch to soften before chopping and squeezing dry. Add to the ground pork and ingredients (I). Blend well. Remember to add the water slowly while stirring clockwise, to make sure the water is absorbed completely.
2. Knead the flour and some water into a dough. Follow the method used in Fried Dumplings to make dumpling skins. Put ⅔ tablespoon of filling in the center of each skin then pinch the edges up to make a boatlike shape.
3. Bring 3 cups of water to the boil. Put the dumplings in, one by one making sure to stir clockwise with a spatula or the dumplings will stick to the bottom. Return to the boil. Add a cup of cold water and cook, covered, till boiling again. Add water again. Repeat twice more, so that the port filling can be well cooked. After the third boiling, turn off the heat. Remove and serve.

Notes:
1. Turnip, leek, and white Chinese cabbage can be prepared the same as Chinese cabbage, but instead of blanching to soften, you can sprinkle some salt on the chopped vegetable, then squeeze dry.
2. Scalded dough can also be used to make dumpling skins.

燙麵類

Scalded Dough

How to make scalded dough

1. Measure the flour, sift, and then add lard to it.
2. Heat water to boiling.
3. Add hot water to flour and blend with chopsticks.
4. Blend flour with water roughly.
5. Cover with a piece of wet cloth for about 10 minutes.
6. Knead the flour mixture to make dough. It will not look smooth.
7. Add flour or water as needed to make it moderately smooth. Cover with a wet cloth and let it stand for 20 minutes.
8, 9. Knead again carefully. (It is said that the dough will be in its best condition after 300 pushes.)
10. The dough now is ready for making dimsum.
11. If there is any dough left, remember to cover it with a piece of wet cloth, or it will dry out and turn hard.

韭菜盒子
LEEK HO-TZU (LEEK BOXES)

Ingredients:
42 ounces leeks, 1 cup bean threads, 2 soft spiced bean curd, ½ cup chopped egg pancake, 3 cups plain wheat flour, some 160°F water, ⅓ cup oil.
(I) 2 teaspoons salt, ½ teaspoon sesame oil.

Method:
1. Remove old and withered leaves from the leeks and wash clean. Soak the bean threads in water for 10 minutes. Dice the leeks, bean thread, and spiced bean curds and blend well with the chopped egg pancake and ingredients (I).
2. Make scalded dough according to the steps in "How to make scalded dough." Cut the dough into 4-ounce pieces; then use a rolling pin to roll each part into a circle 4-6 inches wide. Spread filling on each piece. (The filling should cover around 80% of the piece.) Fold it up to make a semicircle and trim the edge with the brim of a bowl.
3. Put oil in a frying pan. Put ho-tzu in. Fry over a low to medium heat for 10-15 minutes turning once and then remove when the surface is browned. Serve.

Note:
Instead of frying, you can bake ho-tzu without oil. They will be chewy but not crispy.

蔥油餅
SCALLION PANCAKES

Ingredients:
3 cups plain wheat flour, some 140°F water, 1 cup finely chopped scallion, 2 teaspoons salt, 1 cup lard or vegetable oil.

Method:
1. Make scalded dough and divide into pieces about 5-6½ ounces each.
2. Roll out to ⅛" thick and then brush lard or oil on each piece. Sprinkle chopped scallions and salt on top and roll it up. Close the two ends by pinching them hard, squeeze it into a ball and roll it out again into a round piece.
3. Put a tablespoon of oil in a frying pan. Fry each pancake over a medium heat till browned, (turn during frying,) remove and serve.

Note:
Pastry made from scalded dough tastes crispier.

家常菜餅

HOMEMADE VEGETABLE PANCAKES

Ingredients:
31 ounces white Chinese cabbage, 2 teaspoons salt, 8 ounces ground pork, 1 bean curd, 3 cups plain wheat flour, some 140°F-160°F water, 1 cup oil.

(I) ½ tablespoon soy sauce, 1 tablespoon salt, ½ tablespoon sugar, ½ tablespoon pepper, 1 tablespoon cornstarch, ½ tablespoon sesame oil.

Method:
1. Wash the white Chinese cabbage, removing old and withered leaves and stems. Rub with the salt till soft, and then wash the salt off. Squeeze dry and chop.
2. Blend the ground pork, chopped cabbage, mashed bean curd, and ingredients (I) to make filling.
3. Make scalded dough. Knead till the dough is smooth and shining, and divide into 5-ounce pieces. Shape each piece into a bag with your hands and then put 1-2 tablespoons of filling in each bag. Close the bag and press each one to make them flat.
4. Put oil in a frying pan. Fry pancakes over a low to medium heat till both sides are browned, about 20-25 minutes. Serve.

Note:
The pancakes can also be baked without oil on baking sheet.

碎肉煎餅

GRILLED GROUND MEAT PANCAKES

Ingredients:
2 onions, 1 cup oil, 3 cups all-purpose flour, 5 ounces ground pork or beef, some 160°F water (optional).

(I) 2 teaspoons salt, ½ teaspoon sugar, ½ teaspoon pepper.

Method:
1. Peel onions and cut into ¼″ threads.
2. Put 3 tablespoons oil in a frying pan and fry the shredded onion till soft. While still hot, mix with the flour, ground meat, and ingredients (I). (Hot water can be added if the paste is too thick.)
3. Put 3-4 tablespoons of oil in a frying pan. Heat slightly. Put 8 tablespoons of paste in the pan and fry till both sides are browned and crisp. Serve.

Notes:
1. This way of cooking pancakes saves a lot of time spent in preparing dough and filling.
2. Eggplant, pumpkin, gourd, string beans, and other vegetables can be used to replace the onion.

蒸餃
STEAMED DUMPLINGS

Ingredients:
13 ounces ground pork, 3 cups plain wheat flour, some 160°F water.
(I) 1 tablespoon ginger wine, ½ teaspoon pepper, 1½ teaspoons salt, 2 teaspoons sesame oil, 3 tablespoons soup stock.

Method:
1. Blend ground pork and ingredients (I) well, stirring till it is very sticky.
2. Make scalded dough and knead to a smooth long roll before cutting into ½-ounce sections. Roll each section into a circle that is thick in the center yet, thin at the edges. Put 1 tablespoon of filling on each skin and wrap it up.
3. Put a piece of wet cloth on the bottom of a steamer, put the dumplings on top and steam over a high flame for 8 minutes. (The water in the steamer should be boiling before you put the dumplings in.) Serve.

Note:
The skin of steamed dumplings is more elastic than the skin of boiled dumplings.

荷葉餅
DOUBLED PANCAKES

Ingredients:
2 cups all-purpose flour, 1¼ cups cake flour, some 160°F water, 2 tablespoons lard.

Method:
1. Sift the flour and mix together well. Make scalded dough and divide into 20-ounce balls and then flatten each one.
2. Brush some lard on one side of each piece. Put one piece on top of the other, oiled side in. Roll into a pancake with a rolling pin. It is very important that you do not let the edges curl up.
3. Bake each pancake in a clean frying pan over a low to medium heat. (Do not put any oil in the pan.) Bake till the color changes, turn, and bake for ½ minute more. Remove.
4. Tear the pancake into two thin and soft pieces. Use to wrap some filling or Peking duck slices, sweet sauce, and scallion.

發麵類

Leavedned Dough

How to make leavened dough

1. (A) Baking Powder:
   It is used to make cakes and biscuits. The amount used depends on the pastry you want to make.
   (B) Yeast Cake:
   It is used to make man-tou (steamed bread), yiu-tiao (twisted cruller), and rolls or buns. 1½-2 teaspoons can leaven 6 to 10 cups of flour. Keep refrigerated.
   (C) Yeast Powder: (in the glass bowl) This is the same as yeast cake in function.
   (D) Two different stages of leavening are shown in the glass and the bowl.
2. Prepare some warm water.
3. Put 1 teaspoon of sugar in the warm water.
4. Stir it well.
5. Put 1 teaspoon of yeast powder in the solvent.
6. Do not stir. Let stand for 7-10 minutes. When there are bubbles on the surface, the solvent is ready.
7. Mix the solvent with sifted flour. Add some warm water, if necessary.
8. Knead till it is dough. Put in a basin.
9. Use your fingers to make some holes in the dough. Sprinkle with water.
10. Cover with a piece of wet cloth. Let it stand for 3 hours at normal room temperature. The cooler the day is, the longer it will take for the dough to be completely leavened.
11. Two hours later.
12. When it is completely leavened, knead till smooth and shiny. The leavened dough is ready now; however, if you let it stand for another 20 minutes, the dough will be even better for making pastry.

小籠包　STEAMED SMALL PORK BUNS

Ingredients:

Some warm water, ½ teaspoon sugar, 1 teaspoon yeast powder, 2 cups plain wheat flour, 1 tablespoon lard.
- (I) 20 ounces lean ground pork, 1½ teaspoons salt, 1 tablespoon ginger wine, ⅓ teaspoon pepper, ½ tablespoon sesame oil, 4 tablespoons water.
- (II) ⅓ cup tender ginger shreds, 3 tablespoons soy sauce, 3 tablespoons vinegar.

Method:
1. Make leavened dough.
2. Divide into small pieces, about 1⅓ ounces each.
3. Mix ingredients (I) well to make filling.
4. Roll out each piece of dough to a circle that is thick in the center yet thin at the edges, and then wrap 1 tablespoon of filling in each skin to make a bun.
5. Let them stand for 3-5 minutes then steam for 10 minutes. Serve.

湯包　STEAMED JUICY PORK BUNS

Ingredients:

Ingredients for filling are the same as for Steamed Pork Buns.
Some warm water, ½ teaspoon sugar, 1 teaspoon yeast powder, 2 cups plain wheat flour, 1 tablespoon lard.
- (I) 20 ounces lean ground pork, 1½ teaspoons salt, 1 tablespoon ginger wine, ⅓ teaspoon pepper, ½ tablespoon sesame oil, 4 tablespoons water.
- (II) 10 ounces pig's skin, 10 ounces chicken feet, some water, 1 scallion, 1 ginger root.

Method:
1. Dice the pig's skin then boil with all other ingredients in (II). Allow to simmer till there are about 1½ cups of liquid left. Strain then let the liquid stand till it becomes jellied. Dice it. Mix with ingredients (I) to make filling.
2. Make small pork buns according to the method used in Steamed Small Pork Buns. The difference between the two is that the filling of the juicy buns is very juicy.
3. Small juicy buns can be served in soup. You can use clear broth, or make soup by mixing a tablepsoon of soy sauce with boiling water, some egg pancake shreds, and preserved vegetable shreds or ginger shreds and minced parsley.

菜肉大包　STEAMED PORK AND VEGETABLE BUNS

Ingredients:

Some warm water, 1 tablespoon sugar, 1½ teaspoons yeast powder, 3 cups plain wheat flour, 20 ounces white Chinese cabbage salted vegetable, or cabbage, 13 ounces lean ground pork.
- (I) 1 teaspoon salt, ⅓ tablespoon soy sauce, ½ tablespoon ginger wine, ½ teaspoon pepper, ½ tablespoon sesame oil.

Method:
1. Make leavened dough and divide into small pieces, 2¼-4 ounces each.
2. Wash the cabbage and chop, and then blend with the ground pork and ingredients (I).
3. Roll the dough into round pieces that are thick in the center yet thin on the edges. Put 2 tablespoons of filling in the middle, hold in one hand, press the filling with your thumb, and then fold the edges up with the other hand.
4. Cover all the buns with a piece of wet cloth and let them stand for 20 minutes. Put a piece of wet cloth on the bottom of a steamer, put the buns on top and steam over a high flame for 25 minutes.

Note:
Steamed buns taste best when they are still hot.

HUA-CHUAN (STEAMED BREAD TWISTS)

Ingredients:

Some warm water, 1½ tablespoons sugar, 2 teaspoons yeast powder, 3 cups all-purpose flour, ¾ cup cake flour, 1½ teaspoons vinegar, 2 tablespoons lard.
(I) 2 tablespoons lard, some chopped scallion, ½ tablespoon salt.

Method:
1. Make leavened dough.
2. Roll the dough out to a large, thin piece with a rolling pin and spread ingredients (I) evenly on top. Roll it up from the two opposite sides.
3. Cut the roll into several sections. Fold each section up from the two ends to make a square.
4. Press with a chopstick in the middle. Cover with a wet cloth for 20 minutes. Steam for 20-30 minutes. Serve.

Note:
1. Hua-chuan should be served while still hot.
2. You can twist the dough any way you wish.

MAN-TOU (STEAMED BREAD)

Ingredients:

Some warm water, 1½ tablespoons sugar, 2 teaspoons yeast powder, 3 cups all-purpose flour, ¾ cup cake flour, 1½ teaspoons vinegar, 2 tablespoons lard.

Method:
1. Knead flour to a leavened dough.
2. Knead to a long roll, 3″ in diameter. Cut into 2″ sections. Let it stand for 20 minutes and then steam over a high flame for 20-30 minutes. Serve.

Notes:
1. It is said that man-tou tastes best after 300 pushes during kneading.
2. Sliced cold man-tou can be served as bread.

銀絲捲

YING-SU-CHUAN (STEAMED SHREDDED ROLLS)

Ingredients:
Some warm water, 1½ tablespoons sugar, 2½ teaspoons yeast powder, ¾ cup all-purpose flour, 3 cups cake flour, 1½ teaspoons vinegar, 2 tablespoons lard.
(I)　½ cup lard, ½ cup sugar.

Method:
1. Make leavened dough.
2. Roll the dough into a piece ⅛" thick and then spread ingredients (I) evenly on top before folding into a strip 2¼" wide.
3. Coat a knife blade with oil and shred the strip. Divide all the shreds into 5 bundles and stretch each bundle gently.
4. Wind each bundle around a chopstick, remove the chopstick and then cover all the shredded rolls with a wet cloth. Steam over a high flame for 20 minutes. Serve.

Notes:
1. You can use a third of the dough to make skin to wrap the shredded dough. The shredded rolls will look like man-tou this way.
2. Steamed shredded rolls can also be deep-fried; then served.
3. Minced ham can be added to ingredients (I).

千層糕

LAYERED CAKE

Ingredients:
5 ounces pork fat, ⅓ cup sugar, 2 tablespoons rendered lard, 4 tablespoons green and red papaya shreds, 2-3 tablespoons raisins.
(I)　3 cups cake flour, some warm water, 1½ teaspoons yeast powder, 1 teaspoon sugar.

Method:
1. Make leavened dough.
2. Chop the pork fat and then marinate with sugar and let it stand overnight.
3. Roll the dough out to a thin piece, brush on some oil and spread a thin layer of chopped pork fat, papaya shreds, and raisins evenly in the middle. They should cover about one third of the piece.
4. Fold one third up, brush on some oil, spread some chopped fat, papaya shreds, and raisins on top and fold the other third up.
5. Repeat step 4 to make a square cake with layers. Garnish with papaya shreds and raisins.
6. Cover with a wet cloth for 20 minutes. Steam over a high flame for 20 minutes.

Notes:
1. Minced ham can be used to replace the papaya shreds and raisins if you do not like sweet food. Remember to use less sugar when marinating the pork fat.
2. You can divide the dough into 4-5 parts and dye them different colors. Put them together to make a colorful layer cake.

破酥包
PO-SU BUNS

Ingredients:
10 ounces leavened dough, 10 ounces scalded dough, 7 ounces oiled dough.
- (I) 2 chicken breasts (boned and minced), 10 ounces lean ground pork, 6 tablespoons chopped bamboo shoot.
- (II) 2 teaspoons salt, 2 teaspoons sesame oil, ½ tablespoon cornstarch, ½ tablespoon ginger wine, 1½ teaspoons sugar, 2 tablespoons water.

Method:
1. Knead leavened dough and scalded dough together and let it stand for 30 minutes. Roll out to a large piece then roll oiled dough into a large piece on top. Roll up to make a long stick and cut into pieces about 4-5 ounces each.
2. Mix ingredients (I) and (II) to make filling.
3. Roll each piece of dough into a round skin that is thick in the center yet thin at the edges. Wrap 2 tablespoons of filling in each skin to make a bun.
4. Cover the buns with a wet cloth for 20 minutes and then steam over a high flame for 20 minutes. Serve.

Note:
Red bean mash can also be used as filling if you like sweet food.

簡易小麵包
EASY-TO-MAKE ROLLS

Ingredients:
2 teaspoons yeast powder, ½ cup warm milk, 2 cups all-purpose flour, 1 egg.
- (I) 1 teaspoon sugar, ⅓ cup warm water.
- (II) 1 teaspoon salt, 1½ tablespoons melted butter.
- (III) 3 egg yolks, 1 egg white.

Method:
1. Blend the yeast powder well with ingredients (I) and let it stand till bubbles appear on the surface.
2. Put ingredients (II) and warm milk in a small saucepan, stir gently, add ingredients (III) and beat well with an eggbeater.
3. Sift the flour twice, divide into 3 parts and add them to the egg batter gradually and then knead to a dough. Do not add any flour during kneading. Knead till the dough is shiny smooth.
4. Put the dough in a plastic bag then squeeze the air out of the bag and tie it tightly. Wrap in a cloth bag and then refrigerate for 10 hours. (The temperature in the refrigerator should be around 40°F.)
5. Divide the dough into pieces about 4 ounces each. Put each piece in a small mold or muffin cup. (Before you do this, coat each mold with butter, refrigerate for 10 minutes, and flour lightly.) Cover each one with a piece of cellophane or wax paper. Let it stand for 30-40 minutes.
6. Remove cellophane and then sprinkle water on each roll. Put the rolls in a preheated 420°F oven and bake for 15-20 minutes.
7. Beat the egg well and then brush some egg on each roll before putting the rolls back in the oven for a while. Remove. The rolls will look shiny and taste delicious.

水蒸蛋糕
STEAMED CAKE

Ingredients:
2 cups cake flour, 2 teaspoons baking powder, 4 eggs, 7 ounces sugar, 1½ teaspoons wine, 2 tablespoons raisins.

Method:
1. Mix the flour and baking powder well and sift twice.
2. Beat the eggs and sugar well. (Beat till some bubbles stay on the beater for a while when you remove the beater.)
3. Add wine, flour, and part of the raisins and mix well.
4. Spread cellophane on the bottom of an 8″ mold and then brush some oil on the cellophane. Pour in the batter and then steam over a high flame for 20-25 minutes. (The water in the steamer should be boiling before you put in the mold.)
5. After 15 minutes of steaming, spread the remaining raisins on the cake and then cover the steamer and continue to steam till done.

Notes:
1. If you put in all the raisins at once, they will all sink to the bottom of the cake.
2. Do not over- or under-beat the eggs.

馬來糕
SPONGE CAKE, CANTONESE STYLE

Ingredients:
10 eggs, 13 ounces oil.
(I)   1 cup all-purpose flour, 1 cup cake flour, ½ cup cornstarch, 20 ounces sugar.
(II) 3-6 vanilla beans, 1⅓ cups milk, ⅓ teaspoon salt.
(III) 1 ounce baking powder, ¼ cup water.

Method:
1. Mix ingredients (I) well and then sift.
2. Beat the eggs well and then strain.
3. Blend ingredients (II) well.
4. Add the flour mixture to beaten eggs and mix well. Add ingredients (II). Still stirring, add the baking powder dissolved in water and mix well.
5. Spread cellophane in an 8″ mold, brush oil on the cellophane and then pour in the mixture, before steaming over a high flame for 25 minutes. Serve.

Note:
A carton or hard paper box can be used if a mold is not available.

開口笑
SMILING MUFFINS

Ingredients:

2 eggs, 1½ tablespoons lard, ⅔ cup sugar, some water, ⅓ cup sesame seeds, 1 pan oil for frying.

(I) 3 cups cake flour, 1 cup plain wheat flour, 1 teaspoon baking soda, ½ tablespoon baking powder.

Method:

1. Mix ingredients (I) well and then sift.
2. Beat the eggs well and add with lard and sugar to ingredients (I). Add enough water to make dough and cover with a wet cloth for 20 minutes before shaping into a long roll and then cut into several pieces.
3. Rub each piece into a ball and roll each ball in sesame seeds to coat.
4. Heat oil for frying to over-medium-hot. Fry the balls over a low to medium flame. (Keep stirring during frying.) Fry till the balls split open and are golden brown and then ladle out and drain off oil. The muffins will taste crispy and delicious.

巧果
CHIAO-KUO (CRUNCHY FRITTERS)

Ingredients:

2 cups plain wheat flour, 2 tablespoons sugar, ½ teaspoon salt, 1½ tablespoons black sesame seeds, 2 tablespoons lard, some water, 1 pan oil for frying.

Method:

1. Knead the flour, seasoning, sesame, lard, and water into dough. Let it stand for 20 minutes and then roll into a thin piece. Cut into 2"-long strips, then into rhombuses.
2. Slice each piece in the middle, turn one end over through the cut to make a braid-like pattern. (You can also overlap two pieces to make the pattern.) Flour lightly.
3. Heat the oil to over-medium-hot and fry the fritters over a medium flame till browned. Ladle out, drain, and serve.

火燒
HUO-SHAO

Ingredients:
2 cups plain wheat flour, 2 cups cake flour, some water.

Method:
1. Mix the flours, and water, and knead to make a dough and let it stand for 25 minutes. Knead again to make it smooth and a little stiff and then divide into 5 or 6 parts.
2. Shape each ball, then flatten slightly and press the edges between the thumb and index finger to make a swirl pattern.
3. Place the huo-shao in a preheated 450°F oven and bake till both sides are browned and the center juts out. During baking, remember to turn them over.

Notes:
1. The crust of huo-shao is very hard and crisp. Those who do not have strong teeth can soak it in soup, then eat it.
2. It is one of the most popular Chinese dry provisions.

油煎包
GRILLED PORK AND VEGETABLE BUNS

Ingredients:
Ingredients for wrapping are the same as for Steamed Pork and Vegetable Buns. Ingredients for filling are the same as for Steamed Small Pork Buns. 1 tablespoon sesame seeds, 4 tablespoons oil, ½ cup water.

Method:
1. Make leavened dough.
2. Cut into small pieces, each 2½-4 ounces. Make buns according to the steps in Steamed Pork and Vegetable Buns. Toast sesame seeds in a frying pan till they smell good and put some sesame seeds on top of each bun.
3. Put 3 tablespoons of oil in a large frying pan, heat for a while and put in the buns. Cook over a medium flame for 2 minutes, add some water, cover and cook for 5-8 minutes. (Remember to shake the pan once in a while so the buns can cook evenly.)
4. Remove the cover, and add the remaining oil. Pinch the buns; if they feel elastic, remove. Another method is to add 1-2 tablespoons of water, cover the pan, and cook till done.

Note:
Both black and white sesame seeds can be used.

油酥類

Oiled Dough

How to make oiled dough

Oiled dough can be divided into two categories: (A) oiled dough and (B) watered-and-oiled dough.

A. How to make oiled dough

(The ratio of oil to flour is 1:3.)
1. Mix ¾ cup of all-purpose flour with 1½ cups of cake flour. Sift.
2. Add 4 ounces of lard. Blend well.
3. Add enough water to make the flour into small lumps. There should be no flour left in the bowl.
4. The picture shows that there is not enough water, so add more.
5. Knead into a smooth and shiny dough. (Because oil and water are hard to mix, the making of oiled dough is very time-consuming.) Let stand for 20 minutes. Knead again. The dough is ready.

How to make pastry with oiled dough

1. Wrapping made from oiled dough is easy to close and easy to shape to various patterns.
2. If you make patterns by cutting, they will look very pretty after baking; just do not cut so deep that the filling shows.
3. Brush some egg batter on the pastry. After baking, it will look shiny. If you put some soy sauce in the egg batter, the pastry will be dark brown.

B. How to make watered-and-oiled dough

Watered-and-oiled dough can be called sandwich dough. It is made by combining oiled filling and watered-and-oiled wrapping.

(1) Oiled Filling (The ratio of oil to flour is 1:2)

a. Oiled Dough Filling
1. Mix ½ cup of all-purpose flour with 1¼ cups of cake flour. Sift. Add 5-6 ounces of lard. 1 tablespoon of sugar can also be added.
2. Blend well. Knead. If sugar is used, knead till it melts.
3. Knead the dough well. Let it stand for 20 minutes. Knead again. It is ready now.

b. Oiled Paste Filling
1. Mix 1 to 2 cups of plain wheat flour with an equal amount of lard or peanut oil.
2. Fry this mixture in a frying pan till it is a little scorched. Add 1 tablespoon of mixed pepper and salt and 1 tablespoon of ground cinnamon.
3. This fried oiled paste filling is used to make shao-ping (baked cakes) and other special cakes.

(2) Watered-and-Oiled Wrapping (The ratio of oil to flour is 1:5.)
1. Mix 1 cup of all-purpose flour, 1 cup of cake flour, and 5 ounces of water. Stir in water gradually.
2. Add 1 ounce of lard. Blend well. Sugar can also be added.
3. Knead thoroughly. Let it stand for 20 minutes. Knead again. It is now ready.

Notes:
1. The purposes of adding sugar are:
   a. It will be easier for the pastry to look browned.
   b. The crust will be very crispy. However, if you make patterns by cutting, the pastry won't look as good when there is sugar added to the wrapping.
2. Artificial color can be added to the wrapping. For example, 2 tablespoons of curry powder can be used to replace 1 tablespoon of flour when making a curried crust.

How to make pastry with watered-and-oiled dough

(1)
1. Roll watered-and-oiled wrapping into a round, thin piece with a rolling pin. Wrap up the oiled filling. Pinch edges tightly. Roll out to a large thin, square piece.
2. Fold one third of the piece up. Fold the other one third up to make a rectangle. Roll it slightly to make it larger and thinner. Fold it up as before. Roll out to a ¼″-thick piece.
3. Roll the piece up to make a long stick. (Its diameter should be less than 1½″.) Cut into 1″ sections. It is ready to be made into pastry.

(2)
1. Knead oiled filling and watered-and-oiled wrapping respectively into long rolls. Cut into small sections. (Pictures 1 and 2)
2. Press a section of watered-and-oiled wrapping flat. Roll a section of oiled filling into a ball. Wrap the ball with the wrapping. Roll into a ball. (Pictures 3-8)
3. Press each ball slightly. Roll into an oval piece. Roll it up. Repeat the procedure once. It is now ready to be used.
4. Roll out to a thin wrapping to make chrysanthemum pastry, moon cake, Soochow style, bergamot pastry, or pork pastry. (Pictures 9-14)
5. The wrapping can be cut to make eyebrow pastry, wheel pastry, shell pastry, or layer pastry. (Pictures 20-24)
6. Roll out to a long, flat piece to make orchid pastry of flying wheel pastry. (Pictures 25, 26)
7. Put pastry in oil heated to 140°F-160°F. Fry over a low flame for about 20 minutes. Remove carefully. Drain on paper towels. Serve. (Picture 27)

Notes:
1. Three different oiled doughs. (In picture 28, starting from the right, oiled dough, oiled filling,

and watered-and-oiled wrapping.)
2. Pictures 18 and 19 show patterns made by two pieces of dough in a spiral. You can also create your own patterns.

How to bake pastry at home

1. If an oven is not available, an all-purpose pan can be used instead. Set both the bottom pan and the upper cover over a medium flame. Heat till water sprinkled on them disappears immediately.
2. Brush a thin layer of oil on a baking pan. Put the pastry in the pan. Put a grill in the upper cover. Put the baking pan on. Cover it with the bottom pan. Bake over a low to medium flame for 20 minutes. Remove the cover. The pastry can be turned over if you did not brush egg batter on it. Cover again. Bake over a medium to high flame for 15-20 minutes. Remove and serve.
3. If an oven is available, bake according to the features of each oven.

Notes:
1. When the cover is removed, remember to place it over the flame to keep it hot.
2. The degree of heat used is adjustable according to the amount of oil in the pastry. When the pastry is very oily, use a high flame. When the pastry is not too oily, use a low to medium flame.

咖哩餃 CURRY DUMPLINGS

Ingredients (for 15 dumplings)
13 ounces very lean ground pork or ground beef, 2 tablespoons oil, 2 teaspoons chopped red scallion head.
(I) 1½ tablespoons curry powder, ½ tablespoon ginger wine, ½ teaspoon white pepper, ½ tablespoon cornstarch, 1 teaspoon salt, 1 teaspoon sugar.

Method:
1. Mix the ground meat with ingredients (I).
2. Put oil in a frying pan. Fry the chopped red scallion head for a while before adding the mixture, and quickly stir-fry till pasty.
3. Either oiled dough or watered-and-oiled dough can be used as wrapping. If you choose the former, do not fry the dumplings; baking is more suitable. See p.57, picture 22 for details.

椰絲雪酥 SNOWY COCONUT PASTRY

Ingredients (for 10 pieces)
⅓ cup cake flour, 1 cup shredded coconut, 6-8 tablespoons sugar, 3-4 tablespoons butter, some condensed milk.

Method:
1. Fry the flour over a low to medium flame till lightly browned, or steam for 2-3 minutes. Remove and let dry.
2. Knead coconut, sugar, flour, and butter to a dough, and add condensed milk while kneading. Knead to a moderately soft dough.
3. Divide into small balls and use them as filling. Wrap each one with watered-and-oiled wrapping, remembering to make cut in each skin, as the filling will swell.

Notes:
Steamed flour makes whiter pastry than fried flour.
See p.57, picture 20 for the wrapping method.

鮮肉酥 PORK PASTRY

Ingredients:
2 tablespoons oil, 10 ounces very lean ground pork, 4 tablespoons chopped salted vegetable root, ½ tablespoon ginger wine, ½ teaspoon salt, ½ teaspoon white pepper, ⅔ tablespoon cornstarch, ½ tablespoon sesame oil.

Method:
1. Put oil in a frying pan and stir-fry till all ingredients are well mixed.
2. Wrap filling according the steps shown in the pictures.

Notes:
1. The ingredients for Moon Cake, Soochow Style are the same as for Pork Pastry, but use 2½ ounces more ground pork.
2. The filling can also be made without frying. Just blend the ingredients well, remembering to put in twice as much cornstarch.
3. The filling can be sweet or salty. You can create your own. See p.57, pictures 14, 15, and 22 for details.

千層酥 LAYERED PASTRY

Method:
Use red bean mash as filling. See Red Bean Pancakes for the method of preparing red bean mash.
See p.57, pictures 19 and 27 for details.

蘇州月餅
MOON CAKES, SOOCHOW STYLE

Ingredients (for 15 pieces)
2 tablespoons oil, 13 ounces very lean ground pork, 4 tablespoons chopped salted vegetable root, ½ tablespoon ginger wine, ⅔ tablespoon cornstarch, ½ teaspoon salt, ½ teaspoon white pepper, ½ tablespoon sesame oil

Method:
Put oil in a frying pan and stir-fry all ingredients till well mixed. This is the filling.

Note:
You can also blend together all ingredients except the oil and use it as filling without stir-frying. Remember to use twice as much cornstarch.

豆沙酥
RED BEAN MASH PASTRY

Ingredients:
See Red Bean Pancakes for the method of preparing red bean mash. Both oiled dough and watered-and-oiled dough can be used for wrapping.

Method:
1. Divide red bean mash into balls about ¾-1⅓ ounces each.
2. Divide the dough into 2-ounce balls.
3. Refer to pictures 1 to 15 on pp.56 and 57 for the method of making the wrappers. Wrap up each red bean mash ball. Bake at 450°F for 30 minutes. See p.57 for details.

一口酥
E-KUO PASTRY

For ingredients, see Pork Pastry.
See the pictures on the right for the method of wrapping.

菊花酥
CHRYSANTHEMUM PASTRY

Ingredients:
See Red Bean Pancakes for the method of preparing red bean mash. Use it as filling.

Method:
1. See pictures 1 to 15 on pp.56 and 57 for the method of making wrapping.
2. Enclose red bean mash in wrappers and then cut a pattern with a knife. (Picture 1 on the right).
3. Picture 2 on the right shows the cut pastry.
4. Fry over a low flame till done. See picture 28 on p.57.

車輪酥
WHEEL PASTRY

Use red bean mash as filling.

How to make red bean mash:
1. Wash red beans clean. Soak in water for 4 hours or overnight. (Picture 1).
2. Bring a saucepan of water to a boil. Add the red beans. Simmer till they are paste-like. See picture 2 on p.61.
3. Put the cooked red beans in a food processor or blender and mash. (Picture 2) Squeeze out the water.
4. Fry the dry red bean mash with lard till it smells good. Add sugar. Fry the mash until it no longer sticks to the pan or the spatula. See pictures 3 and 4 on the right and picture 3 on p.61.

夾肉小燒餅

SHAO-PING SANDWICHES

Ingredients: (for 15 pieces)
2 cups all-purpose flour, 1½ cups cake flour, ⅔ cup oiled paste filling, ⅓ cup white sesame seeds, 7-8 ounces spiced beef shank or spiced pork meat.

Method:
1. Mix the flours together and then add 3 tablespoons of oiled paste filling and enough water to make a dough. Let it stand for 20 minutes and then knead again till smooth and shiny.
2. Roll out to a large, thin piece with a rolling pin and spread half of the remaining oiled paste filling on top. Roll it up to make a long stick and roll the stick up to make a small pack. Roll out to a large thin piece again, spread the remaining oiled paste filling on top, roll it up to make a long stick and cut it into small pieces about 2½ ounces each.
3. Roll each small piece into a circle. Brush with water. Spread some sesame seeds on each piece. Press hard on the side without sesame seeds.
4. Heat an all-purpose pan and brush with oil. Put shao-ping in, sesame side down, cover the pan and bake over a medium flame for 10 minutes. Remove the cover and turn, sesame side up and then bake for another 10-15 minutes. Serve. Cut each shao-ping open from the side and stuff with sliced meat before eating.

Note:
For making oiled paste filling, see pictures B1-B3 on p.55.

燒餅

SHAO-PING (BAKED CAKES)

Ingredients: (for 15 pieces)
2 cups all-purpose flour, 1½ cups cake flour, ½ cup oiled paste filling, ⅓ cup white sesame seeds.

Method:
1. Mix the flours together and then add 2 tablespoons of oiled paste filling and enough water to make a dough. Let it stand for 20 minutes and then knead again till smooth and shiny.
2. Rub into a 1½″-diameter long roll. Cut into small pieces about 3½-4 ounces each.
3. Roll each one into a thin oval. Spread ½ tablespoon of oiled paste filling on top and then roll it up. Press one quarter of it near one end flat, and then roll the remaining part to 2⅛″-wide piece then roll it up to make a square roll.
4. Brush some water on each shao-ping. Spread sesame seeds on top and roll with a rolling pin into a 6″-long, 2¾″-wide oval piece. Keep sesame side down, put in a frying pan, cover the pan and bake over a low to medium flame for 15 minutes, turning at least once.

米飯類

Rice

How to prepare bamboo leaves

1. You can find the following kinds of bamboo leaves on the market.
   a. large bamboo leaves, dry or fresh
   b. brown, spotted bamboo leaves
   (Lotus leaves can be used together with bamboo leaves. Banana leaves and vegetable leaves can also be used.)

Picture 1
Whether leaves are dry or fresh, boil them in water to soften them.
Picture 2
Wipe both sides clean.
Picture 3 and 4
Trim the leaves by cutting off the points and stems.
Picture 5
Put two leaves together back to back. Use them to make tsung-tzu.

湖州肉粽

TSUNG-TZU (GLUTINOUS RICE DUMPLINGS), HU-CHOW STYLE

Ingredients:
10 ounces pork belly, 20 ounces round glutinous rice, ⅓ teaspoon salt, bamboo leaves, straw.
(I) ⅓ cup soy sauce, rice wine.

Method:
1. Remove the skin from the pork belly and cut into 2″-wide strips. Soak with ingredients (I) overnight.
2. Wash the rice, blend well with salt and the sauce used to soak the meat and then let it stand for 10 minutes. Blend again.
3. Put 2 pieces of bamboo leaves together back to back. Fold up a quarter of the way from the base of the leaf to make a right angle. Put 2 tablespoons of rice in and then lay meat strips on top. Put another 2 tablespoons of rice on top of the meat. (Remember to press the rice hard.)
4. Cover the rice by folding over the remaining part of the leaves. Fold the ends at an angle. Wrap neatly and tightly.
5. Fasten tightly with straw.
6. Put tsung-tzu in a large saucepan. Add cold water to cover by 3″. Bring to the boil over a high flame then simmer over a low to medium flame for 4 hours. Turn off the heat and let it stand, covered for 1 hour. Remove and serve.

湖州豆沙粽

RED BEAN MASH TSUNG-TZU, HU-CHOW STYLE

Ingredients:
8 ounces pork fat, 21 ounces sugar, 10 ounces red beans, 20 ounces round glutinous rice, bamboo leaves.

Method:
1. Cut the pork fat into 2″-long, ½″-wide strips. Marinate with ⅔ cup of sugar overnight.
2. Refer to Red Bean Pancakes for the method of preparing red bean mash.
3. Wrap each pork fat strip with 2 tablespoons of red bean mash and form into an oval.
4. Make tsung-tzu according to the steps in Pork Tsung-Tzu, Hu-Chow Style.

Notes:
1. Tsung-Tzu will taste even better if you boil pork tsung-tsu and red bean mash tsung-tzu together.
2. If one bamboo leaf is not long enough, you can use another one together with the short one.

碱粽
CHIEN TSUNG

Ingredients:
21 ounces round glutinous rice, 0.4 ounce sodium carbonate powder, bamboo leaves, straw, ½ teaspoon borax.

Method:
1. Wash the rice, blend with sodium carbonate powder and let it stand for 1-2 hours.
2. Use only 1 leaf to make each chien-tsung. Do not put too much rice in tsung-tzu.
3. Put tsung-tzu in a saucepan full of water, add borax, bring to the boil and then let boil for 4 hours. Turn off the heat, let it stand, covered, for 1 hour and serve.

Notes:
1. Tsung-tzu will look transparent if you add the borax to the water.
2. If you use the brown, spotted bamboo leaves, do not add borax during boiling.
3. To eat chien-tsung, you can dip it in syrup or in a mixture of soy sauce and pepper.

螺角粽
SPIRAL TSUNG-TZU

Ingredients:
21 ounces glutinous rice, ½ teaspoon salt, 6½ ounces red beans (or green beans, peanuts, or black dates), 20 fresh bamboo leaves, 1 bundle of straw.

Method:
1. Wash the rice, drain and blend with salt. Wash the red beans. If you use peanuts or black dates, soak in water for 2-4 hours.
2. Blend the rice and red beans together. Put 2 leaves together back to back. Fold the leaf points up to make a sugar-cone shape. Put rice in the cone, stuffing it in hard. (Do not leave any space between the grains of rice.)
3. Fold the remaining part to make a triangular shape and tie it with straw.
4. Bring to the boil according to the steps in Tsung-Tzu, Hu-Chow Style.

Notes:
1. If you use rice only, the tsung-tzu is called crystal tsung-tzu. To eat, dip in sugar or a sauce.
2. There's another way to eat this tsung-tzu. Let it get cold, remove the leaves and flour it. Fry in over-medium-hot oil till golden brown. Tsung-tzu tastes very good after frying.

粿粽
KUO TSUNG

Ingredients:
6 cups boiling water, ½ cup dried turnip shreds, 8 ounces pork belly, 4 tablespoons dried baby shrimps, 4 tablespoons oil, 4 tablespoons minced red scallion head, bamboo leaves, straw.
- (I) 21 ounces tsai-lai rice powder, 3 ounces glutinous rice powder.
- (II) 1 teaspoon salt, 1½ tablespoons soy sauce, ½ tablespoon sugar, 1 tablespoon cornstarch paste, ½ tablespoon wine.

Method:
1. Mix ingredients (I) well and then stir in boiling water, little by little.
2. Soak dried turnip shreds in water for 10 minutes and then squeeze dry. Cut the pork into large cubes. Soak the dried baby shrimps in water for 20 minutes. Mix together ingredients (II).
3. Put oil in a frying pan. Stir-fry the minced red scallion head for a few seconds and then add the dried baby shrimps, pork cubes, and dried turnip shreds. Add ingredients (II) during stir-frying. Stir-fry for 3 minutes. Remove. This is the filling.
4. Brush oil evenly on the inner side of a bamboo leaf. Fold it up. Put 1½ tablespoons of the rice powder paste in the bottom and then put 1 tablespoon of filling on top. Cover with 1½ tablepsoons of rice powder paste. Wrap it up to make tsung-tzu. Put in a steamer and steam for 40 minutes. Remember to remove the cover once every 10 minutes, or the tsung-tzu will split open.

Notes:
1. Mustard head, pumpkin, spinach, carrot, etc., can all be used as ingredients.
2. You can also use 21 ounces of glutinous rice and 2 ounces of flour to replace the rice powder.

河粉捲
HO-FEN ROLLS (RICE ROLLS)

Ingredients:
10 ounces fresh shelled shrimps, 1 tablespoon chopped pork fat, 2 tablespoons oil, 21 ounces ho-fen, ½ tablespoon lard, 2 tablespoons chopped parsley.
- (I) 1 tablespoon ginger wine, ⅓ teaspoon salt, ⅓ teaspoon pepper, ⅓ tablespoon cornstarch.
- (II) 2 tablespoons seafood sauce, 1 teaspoon salt, ½ tablespoon cornstarch, ½ cup soup stock, 2 tablespoons chopped parsley.

Method:
1. Wash the shrimps. Marinate with ingredients (I) and the chopped pork fat for 20 minutes.
2. Stir-fry ingredients (II) with oil, removing when it comes to a boil.
3. Open ho-fen out to a large piece. Cut in two. Spread the shrimps and the pork fat mixture evenly on top. Roll it up to make two 1½"-wide sticks.
4. Brush lard on a plate. Put the ho-fen rolls on top and steam for 7-8 minutes over a medium to high flame. (Put the ho-fen rolls in the steamer after the water in the bottom is boiling.) Pour ingredients (II) on top. Serve.

Note:
Pork and beef can be used to replace shrimps.

河粉湯
HO-FEN SOUP

Ingredients:
10 ounces shredded beef, 10 ounces white Chinese cabbage, 4 tablespoons oil, 1 tablespoon minced scallion, 8 cups soup stock, 26 ounces ho-fen.
(I) ½ tablespoon ginger wine, ½ teaspoon salt, ⅓ teaspoon five-spice powder, 1 teaspoon sesame oil, 1 tablespoon cornstarch, 5 tablespoons water.
(II) 1½ teaspoons salt, ½ tablespoon soy sauce.

Method:
1. Marinate the shredded beef with ingredients (I) for 20 minutes. Wash the white Chinese cabbage and cut into long strips. Cut the ho-fen into 3/8″-wide strips.
2. Put oil in a frying pan. Stir-fry the minced scallion for a few seconds and then add the beef. Stir-fry till its color changes and then pour in the soup stock. Add the ho-fen and ingredients (II), and bring to the boil. Add the Chinese cabbage and allow to boil for 2 minutes. Remove and serve.

Notes:
1. Ho-fen can be cooked by boiling, stir-frying, steaming, or deep-frying.
2. Chicken or pork can be used instead of beef.

壽司二式
SUSHI, TWO DIFFERENT STYLES

Ingredients:
3 cups cooked rice, 4-6 pieces laver, 20 flat fried bean curds, 2 eggs (Cook it to make eggpancake first, and then cut it into shreds.), 1 large piece of pickled ginger (shredded), shredded cucumber, pork fluff, 1 tablespoon sesame seeds.
(I) 3 tablepsoons white vinegar, 4 tablespoons sugar, 1½ tablespoons water.
(II) 1½ tablespoons soy sauce, ½ tablespoon sugar, ½ teaspoon five-spice powder, 1 cup water.

Method:
1. Put ingredients (I) in a samll saucepan. Melt the sugar over a low flame and then pour slowly into the cooked rice. (Stir the rice loose with chopsticks first.) Keep stirring as you add the solvent of ingredients (I).
2. Bake the laver over a low flame for a few seconds. Put the fried bean curds in ingredients (II). Let them boil for 5 minutes and then remove and squeeze dry. Rub them gently and carefully to make a hole in the middle of each one. Cut each one across to make 2 triangles and remove the soft inner part.
3. Spread rice thinly on the laver. Put the egg shreds, ginger shreds, cucumber shreds, and pork fluff on top and then shape them into a long strip. Use a bamboo mat to roll it up (or use your hands) and cut into 1″ sections. Serve.
4. If you use fried bean curds, stuff each triangle with rice, sprinkle sesame seeds, egg shreds, and ginger shreds on top. Serve.

Note:
Raw fish slices, cooked squid shreds, fried pork or beef shreds, caviar, jam, cheese, and various kinds of sauce can all be used as filling.

台式香菇肉粽

BLACK MUSHROOM AND PORK TSUNG-TZU, TAIWANESE STYLE

Ingredients:
21 ounces glutinous rice, 10 ounces pork belly, 8-10 dried black mushrooms, 4 tablespoons dried baby shrimps, 4-5 ounces peanuts, 4 tablespoons lard or oil, 5 tablespoons minced red scallion head, ⅔ cup water or soup stock.
(I) 1½ tablespoons soy sauce, ½ teaspoon black pepper, ½ teaspoon salt.

Method:
1. Wash the rice. Drain. Cut the pork into large cubes. Soak the dried black mushrooms in water and then remove footstalks and dice. Soak the dried baby shrimps in water for a while. Wash the peanuts and then soak in water overnight, washing again on the second day.
2. Put oil in a frying pan. Fry the minced red scallion head for a while and then add the pork cubes, diced black mushroom, and dried baby shrimps. Stir-fry till the color of the pork changes and then add ingredients (I). Mix well and remove, leaving the oil in the pan.
3. Put rice and peanuts in the pan and stir-fry over a low to medium flame. Add water or soup stock little by little during the frying and fry till the rice looks transparent and sticky.
4. Use brown, spotted bamboo leaves. Fold one-third of the leaf up to make a spoon shape then spread 1½ tablespoons of fried rice in it. Put 1 tablespoon of filling on top then cover with 1½ tablespoons of fried rice. Wrap it according to the steps in Tsung-Tzu, Hu-Chow Style. (But Taiwan tsung-tzu is shorter than Hu-chow tsung-tzu).
5. Steam over a high flame for 1-1½ hours. Serve.

Note:
Long glutinous rice is not as sticky as round glutinous rice.

筒仔米糕　油飯

MI-KAO (RICE CAKE); YIU-FEN (OILED RICE)

Ingredients:
3 cups glutinous rice, 2 teaspoons rock sugar, 3 tablespoons oil, 6 tablespoons minced red scallion head, ⅓ cup soup stock.
(I) 13 ounces pork belly, dried black mushrooms, 4 tablespoons dried baby shrimps, 10 dried or fresh marrons.
(II) ½ teaspoon salt.

Method:
1. Wash the rice then cook in boiling water for 5-8 minutes. Remove and drain.
2. Cut the pork into 1"-wide slices. Soak the dried black mushrooms in water for 2 hours and remove footstalks. Cut into wide strips. Soak the dried baby shrimps in water for 5 minutes. Soak the marrons in water for 4 hours. Remove the skin. Put in a bowl with the rock sugar and fill with water. Steam for 40 minutes.
3. Put oil in a frying pan. Fry the minced red scallion head for a few seconds then add ingredients (I) and (II). Stir-fry till the color of the pork changes. Remove, leaving the juice in the pan.
4. Put the rice in the pan and stir-fry over a low to medium flame. Add the soup stock little by little during frying and put the stir-fried mixture of scallion etc. in when the rice is cooked. Mix well. This is the so-called yiu-fan (oiled rice).
5. Mi-kao is made by spreading a layer of the fried mixture on the bottom of a rice bowl or container, covering with fried rice, and steaming over a high flame for 20-30 minutes. Pour it out upside down. Serve.

Note:
Mi-kao can be cooked only with pork. Sauce or parsley can be added when serving to make it more delicious.

廣東粥
CONGEE, CANTONESE STYLE

Ingredients:
1-2 yiu-tiao, 1 cup round glutinous rice, 2-3 scallions or parsley sprigs, pepper.
(I) 1 salted duck egg, 1 thousand-year egg, 10 ounces ground pork or 1 large pork bone.

Method:
1. Mince the yiu-tiao and the scallions or parsley. Shell the eggs and then crush them by hand. Wrap the ground pork with a piece of cloth. (If you use a pork bone, there is no need to wrap it.)
2. Wash the rice and then bring to the boil with ingredients (I) in a pot. Lower the heat after it comes to the boil and simmer till most of the rice is no longer in whole grains. Remove the pork.
3. Put minced yiu-tiao in a bowl and then pour on the congee. Sprinkle minced scallion or parsley and pepper on top. Serve.

Notes:
1. If you serve the congee by pouring it on very thinly sliced raw fish, it is called yu-sheng (raw-fish) congee.
2. Beef slices of pork liver slices can be cooked in the congee.

芋香鹹粥
TARO CONGEE

Ingredients:
1 cup round glutinous rice or 3 cups cooked rice, ½ taro, 2 tablespoons pork scrap, 6 tablespoons dried baby shrimps or small dried fish, 3 tablespoons oil, 4 tablespoons minced red scallion head, 5 ounces ground pork.
(I) 2 teaspoons salt, ½ teaspoon pepper, 1½ tablespoons minced parsley.

Method:
1. Wash the round glutinous rice and then simmer with 30 cups of water to make congee. If you use cooked rice, just simmer it with 6 cups of water to make congee.
2. Peel the taro and cut into large cubes. Fry till golden brown, remove and drain. Chop the pork scrap. Wash the dried baby shrimps or small dried fish. Drain.
3. Put oil in a frying pan. Stir-fry the minced red scallion and dried baby shrimps first, and then add congee, ingredients (I), and other ingredients. Bring to the boil and boil till the taro is very soft.

臘八粥
LA-BA CONGEE

Ingredients:
1 cup round glutinous rice, ¼ cup black dates, ¼ cup lotus seeds, ¼ cup red beans, ¼ cup green beans, ¼ cup peanuts, ¼ cup lily bulbs, ¼ pine seeds, ¼ cup dried longan, 1 cup sugar or rock sugar, ¼ cup white gourd sugar.

Method:
1. Wash the rice. Soak the above ingredients except the longan, sugar, and white gourd sugar in water for 4 hours.
2. Put all ingredients except the sugar in a saucepan with water and bring to the boil. Lower the flame and simmer till all ingredients turn very tender. Add sugar. Serve.

八珍鹹粥
SALTED BA-JEN CONGEE
(SALTED CONGEE WITH EIGHT INGREDIENTS)

Ingredients:
1½ cups round glutinous rice, about 30 cups water, 1 chicken liver, 1 chicken gizzard, 5 ounces cowpeas, 5 ounces fresh oysters, 1 tablespoon cornstarch, 1 sea cucumber, 2 tablespoons very small dried baby shrimps, 2 tablespoons minced ham, ½ teaspoon pepper.
(I) 2 teaspoons salt, ½ tablespoon ginger juice.

Method:
1. Wash the rice and then add water and bring to the boil. Lower the flame and simmer till most of the rice is no longer in whole grains.
2. Wash the chicken liver and gizzard and cowpeas. Dice. Cook in boiling water for a while. Wash the oysters, drain, mix with cornstarch, and cook in boiling water for 1 minute. Remove the intestinal organs from the sea cucumber, dice, and cook in boiling water for 5 minutes. After boiling the above ingredients, soak them in cold water.
3. Put all these ingredients and ingredients (I) in the congee. Let it boil for 5 minutes. Sprinkle some pepper on top. Serve.

八寶飯
BA-BAO RICE

Ingredients:
2 cups round glutinous rice, ¼ cup rock sugar, 1⅔ cups water, ½ cup lotus seeds, ½ cup gingkos, ½ cup sweet peas, ½ cup black dates, 6 tablespoons lard, ½ cup green and red papaya shreds, ½ cup dried longans, ½ cup raisins, ½ cup sweet preserves.
(I) ⅓ teaspoon sweet osmanthus sauce, 1½ cups water, 1 tablespoon cornstarch.

Method:
1. Wash the rice and then put the rice, rock sugar, and water in an electric rice cooker. Steam, and then blend with lard while still hot.
2. Soak the lotus seeds, gingkos, sweet peas, and black dates in water for 2 hours.
3. Brush a layer of lard all over the inside of a large soup bowl. Arrange the lotus seeds, gingkos, papaya shreds, etc., on the bottom to make a pattern and then spread ½ cup of cooked rice evenly on top. Put red bean mash in the middle and cover with the remaining cooked rice. Pour a tablespoon of lard on top. Put in a steamer and steam for 40 minutes. Remove and unmold upside down onto a plate.
4. Bring ingredients (I) to the boil. Pour over Ba-Bao Rice. Serve.

甜米糕
SWEET MI-KAO (SWEET RICE CAKE)

Ingredients:
3 cups round glutinous rice, ½ cup brown sugar, 2½ cups water, 6 tablespoons lard, ½ teaspoon sweet osmanthus sauce, 3 tablespoons raisins

Method:
1. Wash the rice and mix it with the brown sugar and then put it in an electric cooker to steam. Add the lard and osmanthus sauce while still hot and blend well.
2. Put the cooked rice in square mold. Press the rice to make it even. Sprinkle the raisins on top. Allow to stand and then cut into pieces when cold.

碗粿

RICE PUDDING IN BOWL

Ingredients:
6 cups boiling water, 21 ounces rice powder, 10 ounces pork belly, 4 tablespoons dried baby shrimps, several dried black mushrooms, 1 tablespoon lard or oil, 4 tablespoons oil, 4 tablespoons minced red scallion head.

(I) 3 tablespoons soy sauce, ½ tablespoon rock sugar, ½ teaspoon salt, ½ tablespoon ginger wine, ⅔ teaspoon pepper.

Method:
1. Add the boiling water to the rice powder little by little, stirring well to make a thick paste.
2. Dice the pork belly. Soak the dried baby shrimps in water for 10 minutes and dice. Reserve the water used to soak the shrimps. Remove the footstalks from the dried black mushrooms and soak the caps in water for 2 hours. Dice. Brush lard or oil evenly on the inside of 6-8 Chinese rice bowls.
3. Put oil in a frying pan. Fry the minced red scallion head till browned and then add all dice and ingredients (I) and stir-fry till cooked.
4. Pour the rice paste into each bowl. (Fill 70%-80% of each bowl.) Spread the cooked dice evenly on top of each bowl.
5. Put in a steamer and steam for 15-20 minutes. Open the cover once in a while to let out some hot air during steaming, or it will look ugly after it is cooked.

Note:
Shrimps or fish slices can be used to replace the pork. You can also make sweet rice pudding by mixing rice powder with brown sugar syrup.

發糕

LEAVENED RICE CAKE

Ingredients:
21 ounces rice powder, 5 ounces cake flour, ½ tablespoon baking soda, ⅔ cup sugar or brown sugar, 3 cups water.

Method:
1. Mix the rice powder, flour, and baking soda. Sift. Mix the sugar with water and stir until the sugar melts. Pour in the mixed powder to make a paste and allow to stand for 15 minutes.
2. Pour the paste into rice bowls, filling about 70% of each bowl. You can also use paper molds to make different patterns.
3. Put in a steamer and steam over a high flame for 15 minutes.

Notes:
1. To make salted leavened rice cake, you can use smoked pork cubes and dried baby shrimps instead of sugar.
2. Cocoa or cherry juice can be added when making sweet leavened rice cake.
3. Do not make the paste too thin. The paste is thick enough when it is hard to stir with a chopstick.

HOT RICE NOODLES, CHIANG-HSI STYLE

Ingredients:
1 pack of Chiang-Hsi rice noodles, ½ cabbage, ½ cup shredded pork, 2 tablespoons small dried fish, several chili peppers, 6 tablespoons oil, ⅔ cup soup stock or water.
(I) ½ tablespoon soy sauce, ¼ teaspoon five-spice powder, 1 teaspoon cornstarch, ⅓ tablespoon wine.
(II) 1½ teaspoons salt.

Method:
1. Soak the rice noodles in hot water for 20 minutes. Stir them loose by hand.
2. Remove old leaves from the cabbage and wash clean before cutting into wide shreds. Marinate the pork shreds with ingredients (I) for 10 minutes. Wash the small dried fish. Drain. Cut the chili peppers into wide shreds.
3. Put oil in a frying pan. Fry the small dried fish and chili pepper shreds first for a few seconds and then add the pork shreds. Stir-fry till the color of the pork changes and add soup stock or water and cabbage. Stir-fry over a high flame till the cabbage turns soft and then put the rice noodles and ingredients (II) in. Mix well. Cover the pan and simmer for 3-5 minutes and then uncover and stir-fry for a short while. Serve.

STIR-FRIED RICE NOODLES, TAIWANESE STYLE

Ingredients:
⅓ cup shredded pork, some leeks, 5 ounces bean sprouts, 2 tablespoons pork scrap, 1 pack of thin rice noodles, 6 tablespoons oil, 4 tablespoons minced red scallion head, ½ cup soup stock.
(I) ⅓ tablespoon soy sauce, 2 teaspoons cornstarch, ⅓ tablespoon ginger wine.
(II) 1 teaspoon salt, 1½ tablespoons soy sauce.

Method:
1. Marinate the shredded pork with ingredients (I) for 20 minutes.
2. Wash the leeks. Cut into 1″ sections. Remove the root parts from the bean sprouts and then wash clean. Chop the pork scrap. Soak rice noodles for a short while in water, remove and drain.
3. Put oil in a frying pan. Fry the minced scallion head for a few seconds and then stir-fry the shredded pork for a while. Add the chopped scrap, bean sprouts, soup stock, rice noodles, and ingredients (II), and stir-fry over a high flame. Add the leeks when there is no more juice left and stir-fry for a short while. Serve.

鹹味米台目
SALTED MI-TAI-MU

Ingredients:
10 ounces green-stemmed flat cabbage, 8 ounces lean shredded pork, 4 tablespoons oil, ½ tablespoon chopped garlic, 3 tablespoons small dried fish, 8 cups soup stock, 2½ pounds mi-tai-mu.
(I) 2 tablespoons soy sauce, 2 teaspoons ginger wine.
(II) 1½ teaspoons salt.

Method:
1. Wash the green-stemmed flat cabbage and then cut into long strips. Marinate the shredded pork with ingredients (I) for 10 minutes.
2. Put oil in a frying pan. Fry the chopped garlic and the small dried fish till they smell good and then add the pork shreds. Stir-fry till the color of the pork changes, and then add the soup stock, mi-tai-mu, and ingredients (II). Bring to a boil. Put in the green-stemmed flat cabbage, and allow to boil for 1 ½ minutes. Serve.

Note:
Mi-tai-mu are a kind of noodles made from rice powder. They are fresh and wet. Rice noodles are usually dried and can be preserved for a long time.

什錦米台目冰
MI-TAI-MU AND ASSORTED INGREDIENTS WITH CHOPPED ICE

Ingredients:
½ cup sugar, 6 cups water, 21 ounces mi-tai-mu, 3 tablespoons fen-yuan, 3 tablespoons yu-yuan, 3 tablespoons kuo-yuan, 2 cups chopped ice.

Method:
Melt the sugar in water. (Bring the water to the boil first.) Let it cool. Add all the other ingredients. Serve.

Note:
You can buy already-cooked fen-yuan, yu-yuan and kuo-yuan. Fen-yuan are the small balls made from cornstarch or potato powder, very tender after cooked. Yu-yuan are the small balls made from taro powder and potato powder. The color is light purple. Kuo-yuan are made from rice powder. Their color is light yellow.

糖年糕

SWEET NIEN-KAO (YEAR CAKE)

Ingredients:
6-7 cups water, 21 ounces brown sugar, 10 black dates, 32 ounces glutinous rice powder, 10 ounces tsai-lai rice powder, 8 tablespoons lard

Method:
1. Put the water in a small saucepan, add the sugar and bring to the boil to melt the sugar. Wash the dates and soak them in water for 4 hours.
2. Mix the rice powders together. Pour the sugar syrup into the powder little by little, stirring till it is well mixed and then add 6 tablespoons of lard and blend well.
3. Put a piece of cellophane in a steamer. (Brush a layer of oil on the cellophane first.) Pour the thick paste on the cellopane, garnish with dates on top and steam over a high flame for 2-4 hours. (The water in the steamer should be boiling before you pour in the paste.)

Notes:
1. You can stick a chopstick into nien-kao; if no juice sticks to the chopstick, nien-kao is fully cooked.
2. Put enough water in the steamer. If you add water during the steaming, nien-kao will not taste good.
3. Nien-kao is more elastic if tsai-lai rice powder is used. If you like sticky nien-kao, do not add any tsai-lai rice powder; use glutinous rice powder only.

廣式蘿蔔糕

TURNIP CAKE, CANTONESE STYLE

Ingredients:
6 tablespoons lard, ⅓ cup chopped dried baby shrimps, 4 pounds white turnip, 3 teaspoons salt, 1-1½ cups water, 21 ounces tsai-lai rice powder, 1 tablespoon chopped parsley.
(I) ⅓ cup chopped smoked pork, ⅓ cup chopped smoked sausage, 1½ teaspoons white pepper, 1 tablespoon sugar.

Method:
1. Put oil in a frying pan. Heat for a while. Fry the chopped dried baby shrimps till they smell good and then add the turnip shreds and salt. Let the mixture boil till it turns pastelike and then add ingredients (I). Mix well. Turn off the heat.
2. Add water to the tsai-lai rice powder to make a thick paste and mix it with the turnip paste.
3. Brush oil on a piece of cellophane. Put it in a steamer. Pour the mixed paste on the cellophane and steam over a high flame for 2 hours. Remove, and put it in a drafty place to cool down. Sprinkle the chopped parsley on top when it is cold. Slice and then serve. (You can also grill the slices, and then serve.)

Notes:
1. The chopped smoked pork and sausage should be in ¼" cubes.
2. Use juicy turnips with a thin skin.
3. Stick a chopstick into the turnip cake to check on whether it is cooked.

煎年糕

GRILLED NIEN-KAO

Ingredients:
6 tablespoons oil, 2 tablespoons water, minced parsley, 21 ounces nien-kao.

Dipping (I):
1 tablespoon minced garlic, 3 tablespoons soy sauce, ½ tablespoon chili pepper sauce.

Dipping (II):
2 tablespoons sweet and hot sauce, 1 tablespoon thick soy sauce, 1 tablespoon seafood sauce.

Method:
1. Mix ingredients in dipping (I) together. Put 2 tablespoons of oil in a frying pan. Put dipping (II) and the water in and let it boil for 1 minute. Sprinkle the minced parsley on top.
2. Put oil in a clean frying pan. Arrange the nien-kao slices in the pan and grill over a medium heat till both sides are browned. Remove. Dip in the two dressing to eat.

Note:
It is very delicious to wrap jam or sauce with grilled nien-kao.

素炒年糕

STIR-FRIED NIEN-KAO WITH VEGETABLE

Ingredients:
26 ounces nien-kao, 20 dried black mushrooms, 10 ounces green-stemmed flat cabbage, 4 tablespoons oil, 3 tablespoons soy sauce, ½ tablespoon sugar, ½ cup soup stock, ½ teaspoon salt, sesame oil.

Method:
1. Slice the nien-kao on a slant. Remove the footstalks from the black mushrooms. Soak in water for 2 hours. Wash the cabbage clean. Cut into 1" sections.
2. Put oil in a frying pan. Stir-fry the black mushrooms for a while and then add soy sauce, sugar, and soup stock. Cover the pan and boil for 1-2 minutes. Put the nien-kao, the cabbage, and other ingredients in the pan and stir-fry till the cabbage turns soft. Serve.

桂花酒釀湯圓
TANG-YUAN (BALLS OF GLUTINOUS RICE) IN OSMANTHUS AND FERMENTED RICE SOUP

炸糯米丸子
FRIED GLUTINOUS RICE BALLS

Ingredients:
1-2 cups water, 21 ounces glutinous rice powder, 1 cup red bean mash, 1 cup sesame powder, ⅓ cup sugar, lard.

(I) 1½ tablespoons sweet fermented rice, ¼ teaspoon osmanthus sauce, 1 egg, 1½ tablespoons sugar (for one serving).

Method:
1. Add some water to 3-4 tablespoons of rice powder to make a dough. Put it in a small saucepan of boiling water and let it boil till cooked. Ladle out and put into the rice powder. Add water and knead to dough. This dough is used for wrapping.
2. A. Red bean mash filling: See Red Bean Pancakes for how to prepare red bean mash.
   B. Sesame filling: Mix sesame powder, sugar, and lard together to make dough. Divide into small pieces. Rub each into a ¾"-diameter ball. The sesame balls are used as filling.
3. Wrap filling with wrappers made from the glutinous rice powder dough. You can shape it to any patterns you like. Tang-yuan can also be made by putting the wet filling balls in dry glutinous rice powder on a large tray and shaking the tray to let the rice powder coat the filling heavily. This is called shou-yiao-tang-yuan "made by hands and shaking."
4. Bring a saucepan of water to the boil. Put in the tang-yuan (also called yuan-hsiao). Remember to stir once in a while to keep the tang-yuan from sticking to the bottom of the pan. Simmer over a low to medium flame for 3 minutes and then raise the flame to high and let it boil till the tang-yuan are floating. Ladle out.
5. Bring ingredients (I) to a boil with a cup of water. Put in the cooked tang-yuan. This is the Tang-Yuan in Osmanthus and Fermented Rice Soup.
6. Put some artificial color in the rice powder, and then make it into small balls. These balls are called yuan-tzu. Yuan-tzu can be served salty or sweet.
7. Besides boiling, both tang-yuan and yuan-tzu can be coated with flour, and then fried in over-medium-hot oil till scorched, drained and served. Dip in honey, sugar, or sweet sauce to eat.

鮮肉湯圓　圓仔湯
PORK TANG-YUAN　YUAN-TZU SOUP

Ingredients:

7-8 ounces lean ground pork, 10 ounces spinach or tung-hao, 26 ounces dough of glutinous rice powder, 8 cups clear soup stock.

(I)　1 teaspoon salt, ⅓ teaspoon pepper, ½ tablespoon ginger wine.

(II)　1 teaspoon salt, some sesame oil.

Method:

1. Mix the ground pork with ingredients (I). Wash the spinach and cut into 1" sections.
2. Divide the dough into 1 ounce small balls. Press into a round wrapper with your hands and then put ½ tablespoon of pork filling in each wrapper.
3. Bring clear soup stock to the boil and put in the tang-yuan. Let them boil till they are floating, and then add the spinach. Let it boil for 1½ minutes and then and ingredients (II). Serve.

Note:

This is the method for making Pork Tang-Yuan. Yuan-Tzu are small Tang-Yuan without stuffing. To make Yuan-Tzu Soup, just follow step 3.

魷魚羹

SQUID BROTH

Ingredients:
13 ounces fish paste, 1 large soaked squid, 6 cups clear soup stock, 3 tablespoons stock fish, 3 tablespoons bamboo shoot shreds, 3 tablespoons fungus shreds, 3 tablespoons carrot shreds, 3 tablespoons shredded pork, 4 tablespoons cornstarch paste, 2 tablespoons chopped parsley.
- (I) ½ tablespoon ginger wine, 2 tablespoons chopped celery, ½ teaspoon salt, 1 teaspoon sugar, ½ teaspoon pepper.
- (II) 1 teaspoon salt, ½ tablespoon soy sauce.
- (III) 3 tablespoons sesame oil, 2 tablespoons black vinegar.

Method:
1. Blend the fish paste well with ingredients (I). Cut the squid into wide strips and wipe them dry; add them to the fish paste and blend well.
2. Put tablespoon after tablespoon of the fish paste into a saucepan of boiling water. Let it boil till all the pieces turn hard and are floating. Ladle out.
3. Bring the clear soup stock, stock fish, and ingredients (II) to the boil. Let it boil for 3 minutes and then put in all kinds of shreds and the fish-paste-coated squid. Bring to the boil and keep boiling for 1 to 2 minutes. Add the cornstarch paste to make the soup thick. Remove. Add ingredients (III) and the chopped parsley. Serve.

Note:
Pork broth can also be cooked according to above steps. Use fish-paste-coated pork instead.

炸蚵餅

FRIED OYSTER PATTY

Ingredients:
10 ounces fresh oyster, ½ tablespoon cornstarch, 21 ounces leeks, ¼ cup chopped cabbage, 5 ounces lean ground pork, 2 cups all-purpose flour, ⅔ teaspoon salt, a pan of oil for frying.
- (I) ½ teaspoon salt, ½ teaspoon pepper.
- (II) 1 tablespoon chopped garlic, 3 tablespoons soy sauce, 1 tablespoon sweet and hot sauce.

Method:
1. Wash the oyster, drain, and then blend with the cornstarch.
2. Wash the leeks. Dice. Mix the chopped leeks and cabbage with the oysters, pork, and ingredients (I) to make filling.
3. Make a thick paste by mixing flour, salt, and some water.
4. Put about 1 tablespoon of the flour batter in a large ladle. Put 3 tablespoons of filling on top and then put a layer of flour paste on top to cover the filling.
5. Heat oil for frying to very hot. Put in the ladle and fry for 5 minutes. The patty will look scorched by then. Tip the patty out carefully, fry for a short while, ladle out and drain. Dip in ingredients (II) to eat.

Note:
You can choose any ingredients you like to make filling.

糖蕃薯

SWEET POTATO IN SUGAR SYRUP

Ingredients:
2½ pounds sweet potatoes.
(I) 10 ounces brown sugar, 4 ounces sugar, 2 tablespoons malt sugar or 2-3 tablespoons rock sugar, ½ cup water, 3 tablespoons oil.

Method:
1. Peel the sweet potatoes and cut into pieces 2″ wide and 3″ long. Wash clean, and drain.
2. Put ingredients (I) in a saucepan and bring to the boil. When the sugar is melted, add the sweet potatoes and simmer over a low flame till they look transparent and shiny. Serve.

Notes:
1. Bananas, pineapples, apples, pears, etc., can all be cooked in this way. If the fruit you use is sour, add more sugar.
2. When boiling, do not stir too hard, or you will mash the sweet potatoes.
3. Sweet potato can also be cooked by coating with flour paste, then frying.

海鮮捲

SEAFOOD ROLLS

Ingredients:
6-8 pieces of wet bean curd skin, 2 tablespoons flour, 2 tablepspoons water, 13-21 ounces fresh oysters (shelled), 10 ounces bean sprouts, 3-5 tablespoons pork cubes, 3-5 tablespoons chopped celery, ½ teaspoon salt, ½ teaspoon xanthoxylum seed powder, a pan of oil for frying, 2 tablespoons oil, ½ tablespoon chopped garlic.
(I) 1 tablespoon seafood sauce, 3 tablespoons ketchup, 2 tablespoons sugar, 2 tablespoons vinegar, 2 teaspoons cornstarch, 4 tablespoons water.

Method:
1. Cut each bean curd skin into 2 or 3 parts. Mix the flour with water to make a thick paste.
2. Wash the oysters and drain. Wash the bean sprouts and drain. Mix the oysters, bean sprouts, pork cubes, chopped celery, salt, and xanthoxylum seed powder to make a filling.
3. Wrap 2 tablespoons of filling with a piece of bean curd skin. Shape it into a long roll and seal the roll with flour paste. Put in over-medium-hot oil and fry till scorched; then ladle out and drain.
4. Put 2 tablespoons of oil in a frying pan. Fry the chopped garlic till it smells good and then add ingredients (I). Bring to the boil and then pour it on the fried seafood rolls. Serve.

Notes:
1. Shelled shrimps can be used as a filling.
2. Fry the roll immediately after you make it. Remember to turn each roll from side to side during frying. Keep the flame over-medium-high.
3. Spring roll skin can be used to replace bean curd skin, but rolls wrapped with spring roll skin have to be fried twice. First, fry them in over-medium-hot oil for 7-8 minutes. Then heat the oil to boiling hot, put the rolls back in, and fry for 1-2 minutes.

油豆腐細粉

YIU-TOU FU (FRIED BEAN CURD) AND BEAN THREADS SOUP

Ingredients:
2 bundles of bean threads, 6-8 cups soup stock, 4 tablespoons chopped celery, ½ tablespoon sesame oil.
(I) 4 pork-stuffed yiu-tou-fu, 4 pork-stuffed rolls of bean curd skin, 4 egg dumplings or some fish balls.
(II) 4 tablespoons salted vegetable root shreds, 2 teaspoons salt.

Method:
1. Soak the bean threads in water for 30 minutes and then cut into long sections.
2. Bring ingredients (I) and the soup stock to the boil for about 10 minutes. Put the bean threads in and let them boil for 1 minute. Add ingredients (II), bring to the boil and serve.
3. Sprinkle on some chopped celery and sesame oil before eating.

炸龍鳳腿

FRIED LUNG-FANG-TUEI

Ingredients:
10 ounces pork belly, 8 ounces chicken breast, 5 ounces water chestnuts, 1 piece of chu-wang-yiu, 3 tablespoons oil, 2 tablespoons chopped celery, 10 ounces cabbage (chopped), ¼ cup carrot shreds, 1 cup flour paste, 1 pan of oil for frying.
(I) 2 teaspoons salt, 1 tablespoon sugar, ½ teaspoon five-spice powder, ½ tablespoon cornstarch.
(II) 3 tablespoons chili pepper sauce, 3 tablespoons ketchup.

Method:
1. Chop the pork belly. Shred the chicken breast. Chop the water chestnuts. Cut the chu-wang-yiu into 4"x4" squares.
2. Put 3 tablespoons of oil in a frying pan. Stir-fry the chopped celery, chopped pork, chicken shreds, chopped water chestnuts, chopped cabbage, carrot shreds, and ingredients (I), keeping stir-frying till the color of the pork changes. Remove. This mixture is the filling.
3. Wrap 2-3 tablespoons of filling with a piece of chu-wang-yiu. Form it into the shape of a chicken leg and seal with flour paste.
4. Heat oil for frying to over-medium-hot. Fry lung-fang-tuei for about 7-10 minutes. (Coat each one with a layer of flour paste first.) Ladle out. Dip in the mixed ingredients (II) to eat.

Notes:
1. Fish paste, bean sprouts, bean curds, peanut powder, etc., can all be used as a filling. If there is too much juice, add some cornstarch or pour off the juice.
2. The flour paste is make by mixing 3-4 eggs, ¾ cup flour, ½ tablespoon oil, ½ teaspoon salt, and some water.

麻辣粉皮湯

HOT AND SPICY FEN-PI SOUP

Ingredients:
21 ounces fen-pi (fen-pi is a kind of wide noodles made from green beans), 10 ounces pig's blood curds, 3 ounces leeks, 4 tablespoons oil, 2 tablespoons ground chili pepper, 1 tablespoon xanthoxylum seed powder, 5 ounces ground pork, 8 cups soup stock or water.

(I) 2 teaspoons salt, 2 tablespoons chili oil, 3 tablespoons fried chopped preserved vegetable.

Method:
1. Wash the fen-pi and pig's blood curds and cut them into wide strips. Wash the leeks and dice.
2. Put oil in frying pan. Fry the ground chili pepper and xanthoxylum seed powder for a while and then add the ground pork. Stir-fry till the color of the pork changes and then add the soup stock, fen-pi, and pig's blood curds. Let them boil for 3 minutes and add ingredients (I) and leek dice. Serve.

Notes:
1. This is a good dish in wintertime, for it is very spicy and hot. Having it in summertime can help you to sweat so that you will feel good as you cool off afterward.
2. It is suggested that cornstarch be added in winertime.

拌涼粉

COLD-BLENDED LIANG-FEN

Ingredients:
1 tablespoon oil, 21 ounces liang-fen (liang-fen looks like gelatin; it is half transparent and is made from green beans).

(I) 4-5 tablespoons ground pork, 2 tablespoons hot bean sauce, 1½ tablespoons soy sauce, ½ teaspoon salt, 1 tablespoon sugar, 1 tablespoon wine, 3 tablespoons water.

(II) 2½ tablespoons chopped salted vegetable root, 2 tablespoons chopped spiced bean curd, 3 tablespoons chopped scallion, 2-3 tablespoons chopped garlic, 4 tablespoons chili oil.

Method:
1. Put oil in a frying pan and stir-fry ingredients (I) for 3 minutes. Remove.
2. Cut the liang-fen into wide strips. Pour the stir-fried ingredients (I) and the well-mixed ingredients (II) on top. Serve. Blend all ingredients well before eating.

Notes:
1. Though this is a cold-blended dish, do not put it in the refrigerator. Liang-fen will be no longer elastic after refrigeration.
2. Liang-fen can also be an ingredient in soup.

花生湯
PEANUT SOUP

Ingredients:
13 ounces peanuts, 15-20 cups water.
(I) ½ cup rock sugar, 1 slice of old ginger.

Method:
1. Wash the peanuts.
2. Bring the water to the boil, and then add the peanuts and ingredients (I) before returning to the boil, lower the flame, and simmer for 1 hour. Try some peanuts, if they are very soft, serve; if not, keep simmering for a while.

Notes:
1. Black dates, dried longan meat, red beans, etc., can also be added.
2. You can also add 1½ teaspoons of soda powder. The peanuts will be easier to cook this way.

炸芝麻薯球
FRIED SESAME BALLS

Ingredients:
1 red-flesh sweet potato (about 5 ounces), 8 ounces yuan-hsiao powder, 1 tablespoon sugar, some 140°F water, ½ cup sesame seeds, a pan of oil for frying.

Method:
1. Peel the sweet potato and cut into small pieces and then steam till cooked. Mash it while still hot and mix with the yuan-hsiao powder, sugar, and hot water to make a dough. Knead till it is smooth and shining and then divide into several small balls, putting a layer of sesame seeds on top of each one.
2. Put in over-medium-hot oil and fry over a medium flame. Keep stirring with a spatula during frying. After 1-2 minutes, press each ball with the spatula. (The balls will expand to 2-3 times their size.) Ladle out when they are browned on the surface. Serve.

Notes:
1. You can also stuff the balls with filling, and then fry.
2. Yuan-hsiao powder is added to prevent the balls from splitting open while expanding.

春餅二式

CHUN-BING (SPRING ROLLS), TWO DIFFERENT STYLES

Ingredients:
10 ounces tender leeks, 3 tablespoons oil, 10 ounces lean pork or beef (shredded), 3-4 tablespoons shredded bamboo shoot, 4 tablespoons shredded dried black mushrooms, 3 tablespoons cornstarch paste, 26 ounces chun-bing-pi (spring roll skins), 1 pan of oil for frying.
- (I) 2 tablespoons flour, 2½ tablespoons water.
- (II) 1 tablespoon seafood sauce, 1½ teaspoons salt, 2 teaspoons sugar, ½ tablespoon wine, ½ teaspoon pepper.

Method:
1. Wash the tender leeks and cut into 3"-long sections. Mix well with ingredients (I).
2. Put oil in a frying pan. Stir-fry all the kinds of shreds and ingredients (II) over a high flame for 3 minutes and then add the leeks. Stir-fry for a short while and add the cornstarch paste to make it less juicy. Remove. This is the filling.
3. Wrap 2 tablespoons of filling with a piece of spring roll skin. Make rolls 2¾"x¾". Serve. You can also seal the rolls with the paste made with ingredients (I), and then put them in over-medium-hot oil and fry till browned. Ladle out. Drain and serve.

Notes:
1. You can use any ingredients you like to make filling.
2. If the filling is too juicy, add some cornstarch.

天婦羅

TEMPURA

Ingredients:
1 large turnip, 1 cup pig's blood cake, ½ cup each of all kinds of tempura, ½ cup fish balls.
- (I) 10 ounces spareribs, 2 tablespoons stock fish, 1 scallion, 1 slice of ginger, 1 tablespoon wine, 12 cups water.
- (II) 3 tablespoons sweet and hot sauce, 3 tablespoons seafood sauce, 2 tablespoons oil, 2 tablespoons water.

Method:
1. Peel the turnip and cut into 1" sections. Cut the pig's blood cake into 1" squares. Cut the large tempura into smaller pieces.
2. Bring ingredients (I) to the boil. Simmer for 30 minutes. Add all other ingredients and simmer till the turnip pieces turn very tender.
3. Bring ingredients (II) to the boil.
4. You can serve it in soup or dip in ingredients (II) to eat.

Note:
The tempura mentioned here are different from the tempura in Japanese reaturants. Chinese tempura are made by frying the paste of mashed fish and flour.

台式肉圓

JOU-YUAN (PORK-STUFFED BALLS), TAIWANESE STYLE

Ingredients:
10 ounces pork belly, 1 bamboo shoot, several dried black mushrooms, 5 ounces dried turnip shreds, 5 ounces shelled shrimps, 4 tablespoons oil, 8 cups boiling water, 31 ounces sweet potato powder, a pan of oil for frying.
(I) 1½ teaspoons salt, 1 tablespoon cornstarch, ½ tablespoon ginger wine, ½ teaspoon pepper, ½ tablespoon soy sauce.
(II) 4 tablespoons white sauce, 2 tablespoons sweet and hot sauce, 1 tablespoon garlic-flavored soy sauce.

Method:
1. Dice the pork and the bamboo shoot. Soak the dried black mushrooms in water for a while and then dice. Soak the dried turnip shreds in water for a while. Squeeze dry. Wash the shelled shrimps clean, and pick out intestinal cords and drain.
2. Put 3 tablespoons of oil in a frying pan. Stir-fry all the dice and ingredients (I) for 3-5 minutes. Remove. This is the filling.
3. Add 150°F water little by little to the sweet potato powder; keep stirring while adding water till it is thick and pastelike. (It should be semi-transparent.)
4. Brush oil inside rice bowls. Pour 2½ tablespoons of the paste into each bowl and then put 2-3 tablespoons of the filling and the shrimps on top of the paste. Cover the filling with more paste.
5. Put them in a steamer and steam for about 10 minutes. Remove. Let them stand for a while to cool down. Pour it out. The jou-yuan is made.
6. Heat oil for frying to over-medium-hot. Put the jou-yuan in oil and keep the flame very low. Fry till the skin of jou-yuan turns hard and then remove. Dip in ingredients (II) to eat.

Notes:
1. See the note for Grilled Oyster Paste for preparing white sauce.
2. Cornstarch can also be used to make the skin. The skin made from sweet potato powder is very elastic. The skin made from cornstarch is very soft. The best way is to combine both of them. The proportion of sweet potato powder to cornstarch is 8:1.

蚵仔煎

GRILLED OYSTER PASTE

Ingredients:
½ cup oil, 10 ounces fresh oyster (shelled), 4 eggs, 10 ounces vegetables.
(I) 1 cup cornstarch, 2½ cups water, 1 teaspoon salt, ½ teaspoon pepper.
(II) ⅓ cup peanut powder, 3 tablespoons sweet and hot sauce, 3 tablespoons white sauce.

Method:
1. Mix ingredients (I) to make cornstarch paste.
2. Heat a frying pan over a medium flame to over-medium-hot. Put in 1½ tablespoons of oil, let it run all over the pan and then put about 2½ ounces of oysters in. Pour 6 tablespoons of cornstarch paste on top immediately. Break one egg and put it beside the paste, breaking the yolk. Add some vegetables and add some more oil along the edge of the paste and then raise the flame to high.
3. When the color of the paste changes, cover the vegetables and egg with the paste and cook for a short while. Turn and cook for 1-2 minutes. Remove and repeat steps 2 and 3 three times to make another three servings.
4. Pour ingredients (II) on top. Serve.

Note:
Make white sauce by mixing a cup of soup stock, 3 tablespoons flour and ½ teaspoon salt together. Bring to a boil over a low to medium flame, stirring during boiling till it is pastelike.

炸芋粿

FRIED YU-KUO (TARO CAKE)

Ingredients:
1 tablespoon oil, 1 taro (around 8 ounces), 18 ounces tsai-lai rice powder, 3 ounces yuan-hsiao powder, 1 tablespoon lard, ½ tablespoon minced red scallion head, some 150°F water.

(I) ½ tablespoon chili pepper sauce, 1 teaspoon chopped garlic, 2 tablespoons chopped scallion (white parts only), ⅓ tablespoon sugar, 3 tablespoons thick soy sauce, 1 tablespoon clear soup stock, 2 tablespoons oil.

Method:
1. Put oil in a frying pan. Mix ingredients (I) well and bring to the boil for 1-2 minutes. Remove.
2. Wash the taro, peel, and then dice into small cubes (around ¼").
3. Mix the rice powder, yuan-hsiao powder, and taro cubes together.
4. Put a tablespoon of oil in a clean pan. Fry the minced red scallion head for a while, remove, and put into the mixed powder.
5. Add hot water to the mixed powder little by little and keep stirring till it becomes very thick paste.
6. Brush lard on a piece of cellophane. Put the cellophane in a steamer. Pour the paste on the cellophane and steam over a high flame for 1 to 2 hours. Remove and slice while still hot. Serve. (You can also let it get cold, slice it, and deep-fry in medium-hot oil for 20 minutes. Ladle out, drain, and serve.)
7. Dip in ingredients (I) to eat.

炸芋條

FRIED TARO STICKS

Ingredients:
1 large taro, a pan of oil for frying.

(I) 3-5 tablespoons cornstarch, 3 tablespoons lard, 4-6 tablespoons sugar, ½ teaspoon salt.

Method:
1. Peel the taro and cut into large pieces and then steam till it gets tender.
2. Press the cooked taro with your hands to mash it and mix with ingredients (I) to make dough.
3. Divide the dough into small pieces rubbing each piece into a long stick or ball.
4. Put oil in a pan. Heat to very hot and fry the taro sticks till scorched. Ladle out, drain and serve.

Note:
You can make salted taro sticks by adding pepper and using only ½ tablespoon of sugar.

甜冷點心類

Cold Desserts

How to make gelatin and pudding

Picture 1
Agar and fish jelly are the major ingredients for making gelatin and pudding.

Pictures 2 and 3
Cut a strip of agar into 1″ sections. Cut 6 pieces of fish jelly into 1″ squares. Put them in a saucepan with 30 cups of water. Bring to the boil over a high flame. Simmer over a low to medium flame. Keep stirring during simmering. Simmer till both the agar and fish jelly are melted.

Picture 4
Add 21 ounces sugar. Bring to the boil again.

Picture 5
Put a piece of gauze in a sieve. Strain the solution once. Let it stand for 1 hour. It will turn into jelly. This jelly can be used to make gelatin and/or pudding.

Notes:
1. If you use just agar to make jelly, the jelly will be very elastic.
2. Fish jelly is made from the air bladders of fish. If you use just fish jelly to make jelly, the jelly will be very soft and sticky.
3. Usually more agar is used in fruit gelatin; more fish jelly in pudding.

香蕉果凍
BANANA GELATIN

Ingredients:
4-6 bananas, 1 large soup bowl of cold boiled water, ½ teaspoon salt, 1 large soup bowl of jelly, ½ cup fresh milk.

Method:
1. Peel the bananas, slice and then soak in salted cold boiled water.
2. Put half of the banana slices in a mold or large soup bowl. Arrange the slices to make a pattern and pour a third of the jelly in. Wait for a while and then add half of the remaining jelly to the mold. Wait for a while once more and then pour all the remaining jelly in. Refrigerate.
3. When the gelatin is completely cold, unmold it upside down into a plate. Garnish with the remaining banana slices and pour fresh milk on top. Serve.

Notes:
1. Banana slices should be kept in salted water, or they will turn black.
2. When adding the jelly to the mold, you can put the mold in cold water as it will help the jelly turn hard faster.
3. When you are waiting, remember to keep the jelly runny as it will be impossible to pour it into the mold if it has already set.
4. See p.115 for preparing jelly.

鳳梨果凍
PINEAPPLE GELATIN

Ingredients:
1 can of pineapple slices, 1 large bowl of jelly (hot; sugar added)

Method:
1. Arrange the pineapple slices in a large soup bowl to make a pattern.
2. Stir the hot jelly to cool it slightly and then pour part of it into the bowl. (Be careful, not to disturb the pattern made by the pineapple slices.) Let it stand for a while.
3. Pour in the remaining jelly and put the bowl in the refrigerator.
4. When it has set, unmold it upside down on a plate and pour pineapple juice on top. Serve.

Notes:
1. See "How to make gelatin and pudding" on p.115 for the method of preparing the jelly mentioned in the above two desserts.
2. You can garnish pineapple gelatin with diced fresh fruit.
3. Pineapple juice can be added when preparing the jelly.

鷄蛋布丁
EGG PUDDING

Ingredients:

3 tablespoons cream, 6 eggs.
(I) ½ cup brown sugar, 4-6 tablespoons water.
(II) 5 cups warm milk, 8 tablespoons fish jelly solvent, 8 tablespoons sugar.

Method:
1. Bring ingredients (I) to the boil in a small saucepan. Stir clockwise with a chopstick during the boiling and let it boil till it smells scorched. Drip some sugar syrup into cold water; if it turns to small balls immediately, the syrup is ready.
2. Coat the inside of 8 to 10 small molds with cream and then pour a tablespoon of syrup into each mold.
3. Beat the eggs and strain.
4. Bring ingredients (II) to the boil but remove when there are bubbles. Add the egg batter and ½ tablespoon of cream when it is not too hot and stir well, and then pour into each mold. Put the molds in a 250°F oven and bake for 15 to 20 minutes. (Or steam for 20 minutes.) Let it cool, and then refrigerate. Serve when it is completely cold.

Notes:
1. To prepare fish jelly solvent, boil 2½ pieces of fish jelly in 3 cups water. Simmer till 1½ cups of solvent are left. Strain. The solvent is ready.
2. If you choose steaming instead of baking, put the molds in the steamer after the water in the steamer is boiling. Steam over a low flame.

奶油鷄蛋布丁
CREAMY EGG PUDDING

Ingredients:

6 slices of white bread, 6 eggs.
(I) 3½ cups warm milk, 6 tablespoons fish jelly solvent, 8 tablespoons sugar, ⅓ teaspoon salt, 6 tablespoons cream.

Method:
1. Cut the crusts off the bread and then soak the slices in water for 2 hours. Rub with your hands to mash and then wrap in a piece of cheesecloth and squeeze dry.
2. Bring ingredients (I) to the boil over a low flame, stirring. Let it cool down a little bit.
3. Beat the eggs and strain and then add ingredients (I). Stir clockwise.
4. Wash a large mold and wipe dry. Coat the inside with a layer of cream and pour in the batter. Put in a steamer to steam for 30 minutes; remember to open the steamer once every 5 minutes, or the pudding will look ugly. Unmold it onto a plate when it is done and pour honey or fruit juice on top. Serve.

食藝之美
舉箸之樂
盡在漢光

味重油膩的飲食觀已經落伍了，漢光保健食譜系列告訴您現代飲食新觀念——
如何做一個健康的美食家。

現代保健食譜

《高纖維‧低鹽——現代保健食譜》希望讓國人更了解，除了眾所熟知的膽固醇、動物性油脂之外，鈉（鹽）和纖維這兩項一直被忽視，甚而認為是微不足道的營養素，在保健醫學及營養學上卻是預防文明病的首要因素，有其不可抹煞的深遠影響。

白小良　著　　定價：270元

低油減肥食譜

《低油減肥食譜》特別針對國人的生活習慣與飲食口味設計，內容包含早餐、午餐、晚餐與點心四大單元，做法簡單易學，使您也能像營養專家一樣調配出適合自己的減肥餐。

周淑玲　著　　定價：320元

嬰幼兒營養食譜

如何讓您的小孩在襁褓、兒童期、攝取到均衡的營養，並養成正確的飲食習慣，發育得更健全，成長得更碩壯可愛？

本書讓您在調配嬰幼兒的飲食時有所參考。

白小良　著　　定價：270元

健康食譜

本書針對強身補血、美容養顏、減肥、高血壓、糖尿病、風濕病等六大類與現代人最密切的吃補食療問題，提供精心研製的菁華。

壽端兮　著　　定價：270元

蔬菜素菜食譜

本書以簡易的烹調法，保存四季時新鮮蔬菜的美味，為國人提供清爽適口的蔬菜、素菜。更期望您能時時享受到大自然裡原野蔬香的真正風味。

壽端兮　著　　定價：270元

中國藥膳食譜

自古以來，食藥同源，飲食療法是中國醫藥理論中極寶貴的部分。本公司特與上海科技出版社合作，研擬出十六種急、慢性病症適用的藥膳食譜共八十道。每種均有病徵解釋，每道食譜後附詳細的功效說明。

漢光編輯組編著　　定價：290元